COACHING THE MATCHUP PRESS

AGGRESSIVE DEFENSIVE PRINCIPLES FOR WINNING BASKETBALL

Bob Huggins

ISBN: 1-58618-173-0

Library of Congress Catalog Card Number: 99-69031
Cover Design: Charles L. Peters
Cover Photos: Brian Spurlock
Developmental Editor: Bruce Brown

Coaches Choice Books is a division of: Coaches Choice
P.O. Box 1828
Monterey, CA 93942
Web Site: http://www.coacheschoiceweb.com

CONTENTS

We believe the matchup press has become the signature of the University of Cincinnati basketball program. Initially, our matchup press came about by mere chance and a sense of desperation. When we were coaching at Walsh College, our team fell behind in the first half by quite a sizable margin. When we met at halftime, I asked my assistant if he felt we could extend our matchup to full court and trap out of it. His response was "How could it be worse than what we are doing now?" The point was well taken, so with a sense of urgency based upon the halftime score, we tried it and liked the results. The next day we set out to refine the matchup press and turn it into a basic part of our team defense. I do not recommend using this press as a last resort or because everything else has failed. In fact, it can be used effectively at any time during the game to create many different problems for your opponents.

Since that halftime experiment at Walsh College, our press has changed dramatically through the years. We have added many new ideas and also tried to adjust it to our changing personnel, and a variety of strategies opponents have used to attack it. The best thing, however, is that it has continued to be successful with every team at every level we have coached. The athletes have learned to love to play this style because it allows them to use their skills to the utmost. Pressing takes its toll on poorly conditioned teams, slow teams or teams with guards who are not good decision makers.

The press can be used to speed up the game, or to slow it down, depending on what tempo you want your opponent forced into playing. The looks of the press can be varied to increase confusion for your opponents. Confusion creates turnovers and quick scoring opportunities for your offense. In most situations, our best offense has been a good defense. Easy baskets are hard to come by in most games and especially when playing another team that also has a strong half-court defense.

Our belief is that you win games by getting more and better shots than your opponent. During our first year at Cincinnati, a booster asked me if I had ever thought of

just throwing the ball out of bounds and pressing if we needed a hoop rather than letting our offense try to score. He said he believed that we had a better chance of scoring if we could set up our full-court pressing defense than we did to score off of our offense. I don't feel like that was the case, but that particular year he could have been close. I took that as a compliment to our defense than criticism of our offense.

Over the years, we have seen many different styles to break our presses and have developed slides, rotations and adjustments to combat most of them. There will be times when a composed, well-prepared offensive team can occasionally work your press over. On those occasions, the pressing team must be sure to keep the basket area protected to prevent easy baskets and get back into a strong half-court defensive set. While we attempt to create a large number of turnovers with our press, it is not necessarily the most important effect. We are looking for a totally disruptive effect on a team and, at times, its best effect can be the mental and physical fatigue it can cause. We also believe that our presses cause teams to take valuable preparation time specifically for the press. Even if they create something new in order to solve our pressure, it is not their basic attack, and they will not have the same amount experience or repetitions with their new strategies that we do with our pressure.

If you as a coach expect your team to use pressure defense, you must prepare them physically and mentally to be the aggressor. It is nice to have a deep bench if you are going to press, but it is not necessary. Your players need to be in superior condition in order to keep the tempo and intensity of the press consistent throughout the entire game, if that is what is required for the victory. Pressing puts the defensive team on the attack and will also increase their alertness, since they know that if they do not come out aggressively, they can give up some very easy scores. Teams that develop pride in the full-court pressure part of the game often become the highest spirited, closest teams I have coached. They understand the power of the press and how quickly the game can change if they all are working at full speed and together. One player not coming out hard or understanding his responsibilities can kill the morale of the pressing team. Conversely, a highly motivated, well-drilled and conditioned team with an aggressive pressing attitude can totally devastate a team that it may not be able to match up with in a half-court game.

I am confident that this book will help you understand and appreciate the press more. This book will give you some ideas that you may experiment with and try to match to your personnel. In our press, we attempt to create the illusion that people are open, and then rotate to them before the ball arrives. You can adjust and readjust the different ideas and drills in this book to play to your strengths and your opponent's weaknesses. Our rules may be a little different than some conventional thinking, but they have proven effective and may cause you to rethink your defensive philosophy. Thinking is something none of us does enough.

COACH = **C**

OFFENSIVE PLAYER = ◯

SPECIFIC OFFENSIVE PLAYERS = ① ② ③ ④ ⑤

OFFENSIVE PLAYER WITH THE BALL = ♂

DEFENSIVE PLAYER = X

SPECIFIC DEFENSIVE PLAYERS = X_1 X_2 X_3 X_4 X_5

PASS = ---▶

CUT OR PATH OF THE PLAYER = ⟶

DRIBBLER = ⌇⌇⌇

SCREEN = ⊢

OFFENSIVE PLAYER O4 WHO STARTS WITH THE BALL, PASSES IT
TO O2 AND THEN SCREENS FOR O3, WHO USES HIS SCREEN TO
CUT

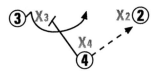

CHAPTER 1

Why We Press

There are many reasons why we feel it is good strategy for teams to use full-court pressure when defending in basketball. We will attempt to give you some of these reasons before we go into the terms and techniques involved in pressing. It is important that each coach analyzes his philosophy to develop theories that he cannot only believe in, but teach to his players. While it is important to be able to adjust and be flexible, depending on your talent and your opponent, it is equally important to have certain areas of your defensive schemes that you keep intact and rely on against anyone you play. For us, the press is a standard part of every game plan. When developing or adding to a philosophy, it is every bit as important to understand *why* you are doing something as it is *how* to do that particular thing. We choose to play full-court pressure for the following reasons.

1. DEVELOPING AN AGGRESSIVE MENTALITY

Teams do not develop a defensive mentality by accident. Much of the mentality of a team is determined by the emphasis a coaching staff puts into their practice plans and what they demand from their players. I personally believe that a player is able to learn and develop as a defensive player much faster than he can as an offensive player. By placing the correct emphasis in your practice plans and by playing those players who sell out, a coach can begin to create the mentality that defense is the one area of the game where he will not compromise. Teams and individuals must have an attack mentality to press. We want our players on the attack when they are on the defensive end of the floor. By starting the game in a full-court press, we can see right away which of our players are ready to play and which are not. We want all of our players to be aggressive defensively every day.

2. TO SPEED UP THE PACE OF THE GAME

Some teams like to keep the game at a slow pace to take advantage of their half-court offense or size. By not allowing them to "walk the ball up the floor" and initiate their offense, we have already taken them away from their strength. Keeping the game at a fast pace favors the team in the best condition. Since conditioning is one of the areas of the game that is in the control of the coach, this is to a pressing team's advantage. When we press and trap, it provides the illusion that there is always someone open, and that gives the impression to the offense that if they "hurry," they may get an easy basket. If your opponents try to speed up and get any easy hoop, they are playing into your hands; and if they don't try to attack your press, it makes it easier for your team to trap without the fear of being beaten.

3. TO SLOW DOWN THE PACE OF THE GAME

Occasionally, we may face an opponent that is a very good fast-breaking team. To get them out of their pace, we will adjust our press to take away the long attacking pass and contain the players in the backcourt by keeping them in front of us. This forces them to work the ball up the floor with multiple passes, thus slowing them down and taking some time off the shot clock. The goal is to not let your opponent play at the pace it desires.

4. TO CREATE OFFENSE FROM YOUR DEFENSE

As I alluded to before, it is easier to score in transition than it is against a set half-court defense, especially against a quality defensive team. We have been able to create more transition situations with our press than by any other manner. We do not need steals to get into transition—oftentimes it is just a hurried shot or a long rebound that allows us to get out and get easy baskets. Often the number of easy baskets one team gets in comparison to the other will be the deciding factor in a game. If we can get a few easy baskets off our press and limit the number of easy baskets the press gives up, the difference can determine the final outcome.

5. TO GET MORE SHOTS THAN YOUR OPPONENTS

As a team, if we can simply get more shots than our opponents, our chance of winning increases tremendously. One method of getting more shots is to eliminate some that your opponent may get. We can do this by forcing them to turn the ball over. Every time they turn it over is one less shot they get. The other way is to make sure we attack the basket and get a shot when we are in transition. The easiest manner to get more shots is to get the offensive rebound. Offensive rebounding in transition has proven to be easier than it is against a five-man defense. All these methods of getting more shot attempts favor the pressing team.

6. TO GET EASIER SHOTS THAN YOUR OPPONENTS

The number of easy baskets you give up against it often determines the length of time you are able to stay in your press. If you are consistently giving up shots that are either uncontested or close to the basket against any defense, you have to adjust the defense, change the personnel, or change the defense. When we are evaluating our press, we keep track of the number of easy baskets we get, compared to the number we give up, to see if we can stay in that particular defense. Our press should ideally create easy shots for us without giving up easy shots for our opponent.

7. TO KEEP THE OTHER TEAM FROM RUNNING THEIR SET OFFENSE

An effective pressing team should be able to keep their opponent off balance and out of their normal rhythm. If you are pressing and your opponent is able to not only defeat the press, but they are also able to get into and execute their set offense when they don't have an early attack, you need to evaluate the effectiveness of the pressure. During the game, you should be constantly aware of the flow of the game and who is controlling the tempo. If you are not controlling the tempo, you need to increase the pressure or change the level of the press, as we will discuss later in the book. Defensively, we want to take the other team out of their spacing, timing and execution. If we are unable to do this, it may be time to adjust.

8. MAKE THEIR "NON–DECISION MAKERS" MAKE DECISIONS

By forcing the ball out of the hands of the decision-making guards and into the hands of the forwards, we can often create more turnovers at the end of the press than we can in backcourt. Players trying to play against us at full speed and making decisions that they are not accustomed to making will be to the pressing team's advantage. This is often a source of frustration, which leads to more mistakes by the offensive team. We will adjust our press against a team that has one outstanding guard, to take the ball out of his hands just to accomplish this goal.

9. DICTATE WHO STARTS THEIR OFFENSE AND FROM WHERE

By adjusting the emphasis or level of our press, we can often determine which player initiates their half-court offense and from which part of the floor. By forcing the ball out of the hands of the normal point guard and making someone else take this responsibility, we may have already accomplished our goal of keeping them from running their set offense the way they want. By forcing the ball to the sideline, or to a specific area of the floor, we may be able to take away our opponent's desire to initiate their offense in the middle of the floor. Any of these small victories by our press may combine to cause the disruption, the turnovers and the transition we are looking for from our pressing defense.

10. BRING THE OFFENSE'S BIG PEOPLE AWAY FROM THE BASKET TO RELIEVE THE PRESSURE

If our opponent has a distinct size advantage, we may adjust our press so that once the ball is entering the offensive half-court area of the floor, it is necessary for them to flash their big people up to the top of the circle or high on the wings to relieve the pressure we are applying to the guards. Again, this strategy will make them play to their weakness and away from their strength. Non–decision makers are now having to handle the ball, and their best rebounders and low-post players are 18 to 20 feet from the basket. Advantage to the defense.

11. WEAR THEM DOWN PHYSICALLY

By constantly keeping pressure on our opponents, we hope to take a toll on them physically. If our pressure is able to fatigue them, this will lead to many more physical and mental errors, resulting in mistakes by the offense. It is a well-known fact that an athlete who is tired physically will make mental mistakes that he would never make if he were fresh. A coach must require a physical commitment from his own players if he is going to succeed at this phase of the press. Successful pressure defense is based on the premise that aggressive continual pressure will ultimately crack the mental and physical composure of the offense. By controlling the action on the full court, we are taking away any normal rest periods they may get by walking the ball down the floor and forcing them into extending themselves for longer periods of time than they would like. If your team is still strong and aggressive at the point of the game when fatigue sets in for your opponent, their confidence will soar, the pressure will increase and mistakes by the offensive team will be magnified.

12. BECOME THE AGGRESSOR; BE THE HUNTER, NOT THE HUNTED

The mental attitude of the pressing team is critical for its success. Coming out at the start of the game by going after your opponent with full-court pressure should put your team in an aggressive, attacking frame of mind. We want our players to compete fearlessly, and pressing often sets the tone for this mentality.

We constantly remind our players about the mental approach to the press and the advantage it gives us. Occasionally, we will ask them "What kind of a defensive team would you rather play against?" Would you rather face a team that allows you to bring the ball down the court unguarded, resting and let you walk into your half-court offense, or a team that is constantly pressuring the ball, forcing you to struggle to advance it with either a pass or a dribble, forcing you into a continually smaller and smaller area of the floor and always having to be prepared for a trap? Obviously, our players see the advantage of pressuring, because they have to face it every day in practice.

13. USE MORE PLAYERS IN ORDER TO HELP DEVELOP YOUR BENCH AND CREATE BETTER TEAM MORALE

Players enjoy playing. They will respond better in practice and be more open to learning if they are contributing during the games. When you commit to pressure defense and the energy it requires, you are committing, in most cases, to play more players. There are obvious advantages to playing deeper into your bench early in the season. You may find a player who will surprise you, build confidence in a larger number of players, develop trust between squad members and prepare yourself for the injuries and illnesses that will happen during the long schedule of games.

14. FIND SOMETHING CONSTRUCTIVE THAT UNSKILLED PLAYERS CAN DO TO HELP THE TEAM

Not all players are offensively gifted, but if an individual athlete will compete by being willing to apply defensive pressure, he can become a valuable member of the team. Most players will be glad to find an area of the game that requires more effort than technique to be successful. As a coach, you will see the pride build for the whole team when all players can contribute to the overall success of the team.

15. YOUR TEAM WILL HAVE THE ABILITY TO SCORE IN SPURTS

An aggressive, pressing team always has the ability to explode for a series of quick baskets. You are never out of a game when you are behind when you can apply constant pressure. There have been times when we are not playing well offensively and are behind in a game, but because of the pressure, we know there is always a potential for a spurt. You never know when the other team will hit the wall and begin making mistakes they haven't made to this point in the game. The belief that we can score in bunches—and you are never quite sure when it will happen—gives our players a mental edge. If you use the press only when you are desperate or behind at the end of the game, you lose some of this advantage.

16. BEAT PEOPLE WITH YOUR DEPTH

There may be some years where your top five players may not be better than your opponents' top five, but if you can play your top nine or 10 against their top nine or 10, you may have the advantage. In these cases, it becomes necessary to "get into your opponent's bench" and play against their weaker players, even if it is for only short periods throughout the game. One of the goals in each game becomes to have the press force the opposing coach to substitute and attempt to keep fresh players in the game. During this time, the depth of your talent needs to step up and outplay their counterparts.

17. CONTROL THE GAME WITH YOUR GUARDS

A good pressing team can neutralize height and control the flow of the game with their guards. The pressure that aggressive, well-drilled guards can produce can take over a game. If your guards can dominate the backcourt and get the ball directed into traps or corners, they can dictate much of the outcome of the game.

For all these reasons, it makes sense for a team to adopt a matchup press into their defensive philosophy. Now, let's look at how this strategy can be implemented.

CHAPTER 2

General Alignment of the Matchup Press

We will start by showing you the whole picture of the matchup press, and then we will break it down into individual parts, including terminology, skills and drills. Then we will return to the larger picture again. We have found it useful for our players to see the whole picture first, so they realize the importance of the drills we do in practice. If we only show them the individual parts, they seldom see the bigger purpose of the drill. If we show them the whole concept first, this causes them to work harder and have a clearer understanding in game and practice situations.

The basic alignment of our press is a 2-1-2, as shown in Diagram 1. This setup places two players in the front court at the free throw line extended, one player near half court and two players in backcourt.

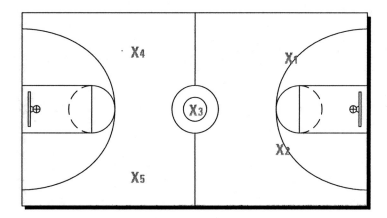

Diagram 1

The illustration shows how we line up initially. This could vary according to how the offense lines up to break the press and what they are trying to accomplish. It is extremely important that each of our defenders knows who he is guarding, or at least who he is responsible for, even if he is not lined up directly beside the man. They need to identify their matchups and get into the correct position as quickly as possible to prevent any direct passes up the court and begin to apply the team principles and press of the matchup defense.

Opponents oftentimes try to distort our press by flooding or overloading one particular area of the floor. One method of overloading is to line up in a 1-4 across the foul line (Diagram 2).

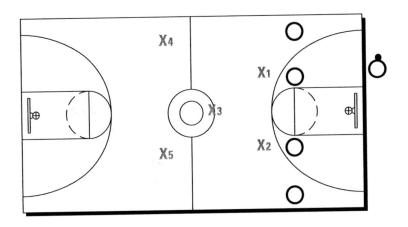

Diagram 2

The second most common method of initially overloading our matchup press is to line up in a 1-3-1 (Diagram 3). In both these instance, we want to make sure our players know who they are guarding so that we do not become too distorted, even if this means backing our press off behind their offensive press-breaking set.

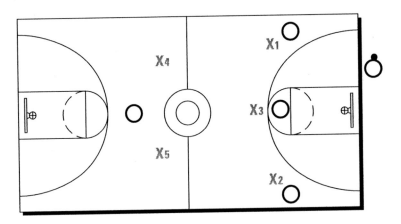

Diagram 3

All press-breaking offenses that initially distort your press will basically end up in one of three alignments once the ball is inbounded. These are:

- 2-1-2

- 1-3-1

- 2-2-1

Knowing this, we pretty much wait until our opponent is in one of these three sets before we even try to guard them. Otherwise, we will become too distorted and the offense will be able to dictate what our press does, rather than our defense dictating what the offense must do. Once our opponent is in the formation that they want to use to break the press, we match up and begin using the principles of the box theory. The box theory is the basic premise for everything we do defensively. The philosophy is simple and easy for our players to understand. By keeping our principles simple and consistent, we are able to speed up the learning process.

CHAPTER 3

THE BOX THEORY

Just as in our half-court man-to-man and matchup defenses, the matchup press is based on the box theory. The box theory is simply a method we use to divide the court into separate segments. Dividing the court lengthwise with a line from one basket to the other creates the first two boxes (Diagram 4). This splits the court into two equal halves, or "boxes," that are used to determine our rotations and slides. The box that the ball is in becomes the *ball-side box* and the other box becomes the *help-side box*.

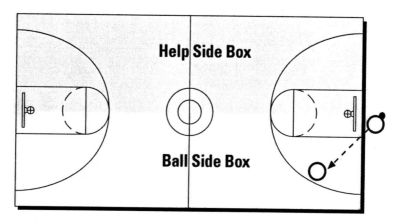

Help Side Box

Ball Side Box

Diagram 4

Once a ball-side box has been established, we attempt to keep it there and not allow the ball to be passed or dribbled out of the box. We do not want the ball to keep changing boxes. We would do everything possible to deny passes going out of one box and into the other, as illustrated in Diagram 5. These passes make the box larger or, even worse, make us change boxes and therefore defend more territory. Defenders must be matched up and in position to deny any direct passes out of the box. Our goal is to keep the ball on one side of the floor and continually push the ball into smaller and smaller boxes to defend.

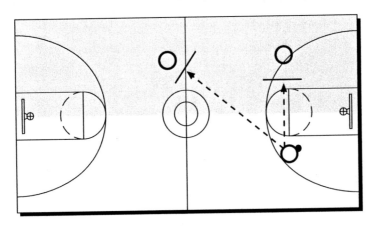

Diagram 5

We would like to keep the ball controlled while being dribbled into a continually smaller and smaller box; but if we can give up any pass, it is one that goes down the court while staying in the ball-side box. Diagram 6 illustrates the kind of pass we can allow, using the box theory. It is a pass that goes deeper into the box and therefore makes the box area smaller and easier to defend. Defenders must be aware as the box changes size, and they must adjust their positioning accordingly.

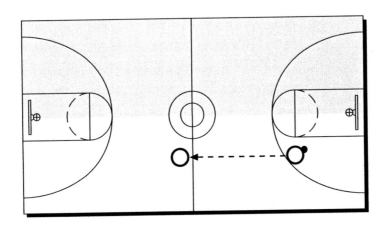

Diagram 6

Diagram 7 shows the positive effect of a pass up the floor that shortens the box. The new box has become the area from the level of the ball to the baseline. The box has gone from half of the court to one quarter of the court, and now the goal of the defense is to keep the ball in the newly formed box.

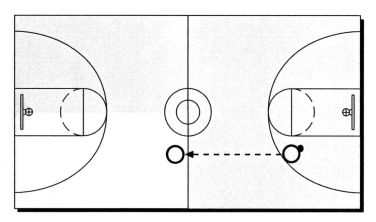

Diagram 7

The reason we encourage the ball to be passed up the floor and farther into the box is that it shortens the area that our defenders have to guard. It also shortens the distance of our rotations and slides. Common sense tells us the less ground we have to cover, the quicker we can get to the ball. In order to enhance this quickness to the ball, the next principle we teach has to do with the help-side defenders and their positioning in the help-side box. We want all of our defenders off the matchup far enough that they can take no more than *one big step* and get a foot in the ball-side box.

Even though we are showing that we allow a pass up the court that shortens the box, it goes without saying that our defenders in the ball-side box will intercept any soft or poorly thrown pass to the player they are matched up with. But if we do allow a pass, this type of pass that shortens the box should be the only one. We want to continue to emphasize the aggressive nature of this press and never send a message to our players or our opponents that we are not on the attack.

Diagram 8 illustrates the positioning of the players in the ball-side box (X2, X3 and X5) and the position of the players in the help-side box (X1, X4). The defenders in the help- side box are within one big step of having a foot in the ball-side box. In this diagram, the ball has been inbounded just below the free throw line extended, reinforcing the principle of keeping the ball in front of our defense initially. X2 keeps the dribbler forced toward the sideline and downcourt in an effort to make the box smaller. X5 and X3 are matched up with offensive players in their area. X1 and X4 are in the shaded area representing the help-side box and off their offensive matchup and within a big step of the ball-side box. They are denying the direct pass to their offensive matchup in order to keep the ball from changing boxes.

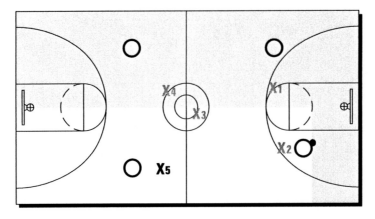

Diagram 8

Diagram 9 shows the effectiveness of only allowing a pass that shortens the ball-side box. As you can see, the smaller the box, the closer the defenders get to the man with the ball. As the ball gets moved down the floor, inside the ball-side box, the help-side defenders (X1 and X4) are moving off their players and are getting closer to the ball. The off-the-ball defenders are closer to the ball and better able to help or trap as the box gets smaller and the dribbler has less and less room to operate and fewer options as the defense closes in. Diagram 9 shows the box getting smaller.

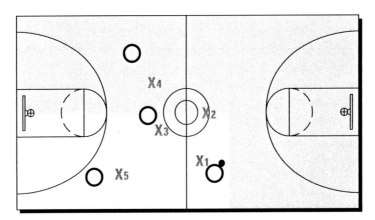

Diagram 9

In our next chapter, we will cover the terminology we use to describe the various defensive techniques to our players. This terminology should be helpful in your understanding of the goals of the matchup press.

CHAPTER 4

Terminology

Part of being a successful coach is being able to communicate quickly and effectively with your players to get them to understand the concepts and techniques you are trying to get them to accomplish. Each sport has its own terminology or language that both players and coaches need to completely understand. Some coaches may have a great amount of knowledge about the game, but unless they can communicate that knowledge to the players, both the knowledge and the time are wasted. The goal is to transform your knowledge into correct physical actions by your players. Coaches who are more successful at this skill need fewer words and less time to get the message across to their athletes.

Terminology is a necessary requirement for successful coaching staffs and teams. Once familiar with the terms and what they mean, coaches can make corrections with single words or short phrases that send a clear message to their athletes and prevent the coaches from having to explain in great detail each time the correction is needed.

The more consistently we use the terms, the less time we spend talking and teaching and the more physical repetitions our athletes get, actually experiencing the skills. You have already been introduced to the terms we use, such as *box theory, ball-side box, help-side box* and *shortening the box*. In this chapter, we continue with the other terms we use on a daily basis to reinforce the correct techniques needed to apply the principles of our matchup press. Familiarize yourself with the implications of these terms and where they fit into the bigger picture you have seen already with the press. You may not want to use the exact terms we do, because you may already have terms that you use and that fit into your defensive system. I encourage you to use whatever terms you want as long as the words translate into the physical actions you are looking for from your players.

ON THE LINE, UP THE LINE

This is a term that we use for the positioning of the players not guarding the ball. In other words, it applies to all the players off the ball. A player off the ball should draw a direct line between his man and the ball and then position himself directly on that line. This theory is in direct contrast to the old theory of being in a "flat triangle" position. The flat triangle is another technique for playing off the ball defense. The off-the-ball defender gets into a flat triangle position by finding the direct line between the ball and his man, and then taking a big step off that line toward the basket to form a triangle with the ball, himself and his man. Diagram 10 illustrates the flat triangle position, and Diagram 11 shows the *on-the-line, up-the-line* position that we now teach and prefer. We taught the flat triangle position ourselves for years before switching to the more aggressive *on-the-line, up-the-line* technique we now use.

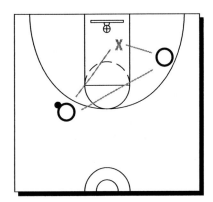

Diagram 10

Diagram 11

This small adjustment in positioning has made a tremendous improvement in the effectiveness of our individual and team defense. We have found that the advantages far outweigh the disadvantages for our athletes. If nothing else, this adjustment in positioning has put us into a more aggressive, denial mentality in our off-the-ball defense.

Here are a few advantages we have found since we have gone to the on-the-line, up-the-line position:

- It takes away vision from the offensive player. Anytime we can take away vision, it helps our chances of being successful.

- It discourages skip passes because the offensive man is harder to find and the pass can be more easily intercepted.

- It makes it much easier to teach players to trap, since they are already positioned in the passing lane. They can take more correct angles in forming the trap, making it more difficult for the offensive player to get out of the trap.

- Because they are already lined up in the passing lane, it also makes all the players one step quicker to the ball, which can allow you to press even with players who might be a step slower than their opponent.

Diagram 12 illustrates players in a full-court-press situation in an on-the-line, up-the-line position. Notice that all players are directly in line with the ball. How far they move up the line depends not only on how quick they are, but also how their quickness compares to the person they are matched up with. Because of the varying degrees of quickness, not all the players would be in the same position up the line, but every player would stay on the line.

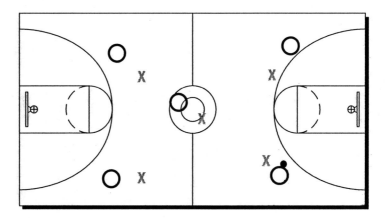

Diagram 12

Compare Diagram 12, where the players are in the on-the-line, up-the-line position, to Diagram 13, where all five defenders in a full-court press are in a flat triangle.

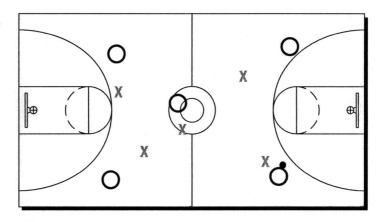

Diagram 13

As you can see, all the defenders in Diagram 13 are closer to the basket when they assume a flat triangle position than when they are in an on-the-line, up-the-line position. While the flat triangle theory is not "wrong," we believe that the on-the-line, up-the-line position is more favorable for both our half-court defense and our pressing defenses.

The biggest reason I hear coaches are teaching the flat triangle is that they feel that their players will not have to turn their heads to see both the ball and their man. From the diagram, this appears to be true. But in actual game situations, these X's and O's are moving constantly. For this reason, we found that even in the flat triangle position, our defenders were having to turn their heads to see both their man and the ball, anyway. We agree that when we use our on-the-line, up-the-line principles, we definitely do have to turn our heads at all times. Therefore, we have changed to the on-the-line, up-the-line philosophy because of the other advantages we have already listed.

PISTOLS POSITION

Pistols position is the term we use to describe the stance of the off-the-ball defenders. The defender in an on-the-line, up-the-line position is in an open stance. This means that both toes would be on a line that runs directly from the man with the ball to the man he is guarding. The player assumes an "athletic position," with his knees bent and his hips low. No matter what sport you watch or coach, you will see the athletic position at work. Baseball infielders, football linebackers, tennis players who are receiving the serve, etc., are all in this position with their knees and hips. It is very similar to the position you are in as you are sitting in a chair or a stool. This position allows the athlete to make quick movements in any direction, an ability that is essential to basketball defense. One of the coaching points you can use to get your athletes in the correct athletic position is to get them to lower their hips by bending their knees, instead of doing so from the lower back. If they are doing it incorrectly, they will look hunched over and not be as quick on their first movement.

The rest of the pistols position involves the use of the players' arms and hands. The off-the-ball defenders point one hand and their index finger at the ball and the other hand and index finger at their man. This action should resemble two six-shooters or pistols pointing at their man and the ball. This technique is very helpful for the player as he tries to keep track of both the basketball and his own man. As the ball and his matchup move, he continually repositions himself accordingly, with his pistols pointing. This hand position should also be used by the coach to tell when a player has lost sight of either the ball or his man. If the player is not pointing at both, we assume he has lost one or the other, and so we make the correction accordingly.

The player's arms should be out from his body at about a 140-degree angle. We want his arms away from his body so they take up more space and can shed any potential screens set by the offense. If the arms are in close to the body, a screener can get into the defender's body and prevent us from making the correct slides and shifts we need to make in our defense.

The defender's head in the on-the-line, up-the-line pistols position is constantly turning to see not only the ball and his man, but also to see if any other players are coming to screen him. We also want our off-the-ball defenders to turn their heads continually so that they can see where everyone on the offense is positioned on the floor. This action will enable them to rotate in a straight line when they change players that they are guarding. As we all learned in geometry, the shortest distance between two points is a straight line, and we believe that that concept makes our players one to two steps quicker than usual in our defensive rotations. Vision again becomes extremely important in determining the overall success of our press.

Together, the pistols position, along with the on-the-line, up-the-line position, are the two most important terms and techniques our players need to understand and apply in order for our press to succeed.

SPRINT TO HELP

Sprint to help is a term we use when it is necessary for our defense—when our players are required to move because the ball has been reversed. The natural tendency for players is to drop more toward the basket than to the ball. We need our players to be able to get back quickly into a new on-the-line, up-the-line position as the ball is swung. We spend a lot of time teaching our defenders to sprint to the newly established help position when the ball is passed from the ball side to the help side of the court. Diagram 14 shows defender X3 sprinting to the new on-the-line, up-the-line help position as the ball is swung across the court. Even though this is one of the passes we attempt to deny, there will be times when we must be able to change boxes quickly and correctly.

The defender must sprint to help, get into the correct position according to the new location of the ball and his man, get his pistols pointed and be on the line and up the line, one big step from being in the ball-side box.

Diagram 14 demonstrates the term *sprint to help*.

- Defender X3 is guarding the man in the ball-side box in an open pistols stance, while staying on the line, up the line.

- As the ball is reversed to the opposite box, the defender must then sprint to the middle of the floor, readjusting to a new on-the-line, up-the-line pistols position off the ball.

- He sprints close enough to be within one big step of the new ball-side box.

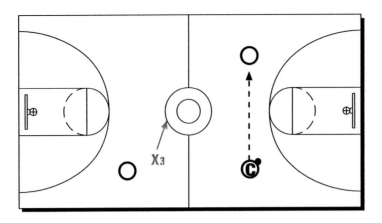

Diagram 14

Drills for developing the skills these terms describe can be found in Chapter 7.

CHAPTER 5

Responsibilities by Position for the Matchup Press

BREAKDOWN BY POSITION

Now that we have discussed why we use the press, the terminology we use, the box theory and our general alignment, we need to begin breaking down the press by position. Each position comes with a variety of responsibilities and requirements that are necessary for the matchup press to be successfully executed. Each player must understand his individual assignments and attempt to aggressively and consistently mesh them together to form a strong unit.

Diagram 15 shows the initial lineup of our matchup press against a 2-1-2 alignment after the ball has been inbounded. We will use this diagram to explain the general physical qualities needed to play each position.

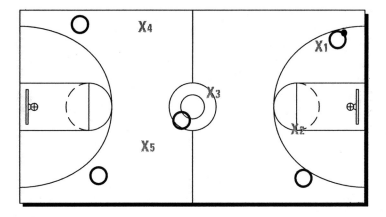

Diagram 15

X1
- This player needs to be a good on-the-ball defender, since most teams will inbound to their offensive right side.

- In order to make passing difficult and trapping effective, the bigger this player is, the better.

X2

- Generally our point guard.

- He needs to be a good anticipator who is capable of making the rotations necessary for this spot on the press.

- He also needs to be a good on-the-ball defender, since the offensive team may be inbounding the ball to his side.

X3

- Generally speaking, this player is either our off guard or our small forward.

- He needs to be a good and active defender who can cover a lot of ground in a hurry, since he is often in the middle of the floor and has the most space to defend.

X4

- This spot is usually our power forward or center, whoever is the bigger of the two players at those positions.

- He needs to be able to actively defend potential receivers down the floor and understand the concept of how far he must come off his matchup in order to be able to help and recover.

- He needs to be able to anticipate and difficult to throw the ball over.

X5

- We most often just place the player we have remaining in this spot after the other position descriptions have been filled.

- It is essential that this player be able to move, as well as read situations from the back spot on the press.

- Since he is at the back of the press and everything is happening in front of him, he also needs to be good at verbalizing to his teammates in order to alert them to offensive player movement.

GENERAL RESPONSIBILITIES OF THE FRONT TWO DEFENDERS

The general responsibility of the two front defenders is to put hard pressure on the basketball. The more pressure they can apply to the person with the ball, the more effective the whole press becomes. We want the offensive player to worry more about the man checking him than where he is trying to pass the ball. When he gets his head down and he is totally occupied by the defender on him, the other defenders' jobs get easier and we have a *great* press.

The two front defenders are also responsible for getting the ball directed into one of the two boxes based on the side of the court. Once they have pushed the ball onto one side of the court, their job is to keep it in that box. While the on-the-ball defender is putting extreme pressure on the ball, the offside defender must deny any pass that would allow the ball out of the box. The on-the-ball defender is influencing the dribbler toward the sideline in order to keep him in the box. If the latter somehow gets beaten on the dribble to the middle of the floor, the offside defender is also responsible for helping him stop the dribble penetration.

We will use two different methods of influencing the dribbler with these two players. They must understand which method of influence we are using against this particular opponent and then work together to accomplish the goals of the overall press. Most of the time, we force the ball down the sideline. But at other times, we will force the ball to the middle of the floor to make the dribbler use a spin move. Later in this book, we will explain in more depth when and how we utilize these two different tactics.

The position and influence of the defender on the ball is really the only major change in either type of press. The rest of the responsibilities remain the same, which helps keep things consistent for all our other defenders.

SPECIFIC RESPONSIBILITIES OF THE TWO FRONT DEFENDERS

Diagram 16 illustrates the position of the two front defenders after the ball has been inbounded, followed by a description of the responsibilities of these two players in this situation.

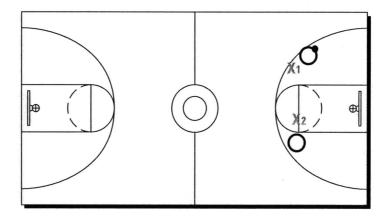

Diagram 16

X1

- Puts pressure on the ball, in this case influencing toward the sideline.

- Pushes the ball to the ball-side box and keeps it there.

- Tries not to let the ball be centered.

- Has his outside hand up at all times to discourage the cross-court skip pass and also to take away the dribbler's vision of the court.

- Never gets cut to the middle of the floor.

- Positions himself so that the only way the dribbler can ever get the ball to the middle of the floor is by using a spin dribble.

- He must stay ahead of the dribbler by splitting the offensive man in half and keeping half of his body ahead of the ball.

- His inside foot is up and his head is even with the basketball so that he can maintain this position.

X2

- Stays on the line and up the line.

- Does not let the ball get reversed out of the initial box.

- Stays far enough up the line to be able to take one big step and put a foot in the ball-side box.

- If X1 is beaten to the middle of the floor on a direct dribble, X2 helps by using run-and-jump tactics (run-and-jump techniques and drills will be covered in detail in Chapter 8).

- If the dribbler uses a spin dribble, X2 also uses the same run-and-jump tactics to attack the ball.

- Once he has used a run-and-jump technique to stop the direction of the dribbler, X2 must then direct him back to the sideline and attempt to keep him in that box.

GENERAL RESPONSIBILITIES OF THE THREE BACK-LINE PLAYERS

The next areas of the press that must be explained are the general and specific responsibilities of our three back-line defenders, where we show how they relate to the overall scheme of the matchup press. Diagram 17 shows the initial alignment after the ball has been inbounded.

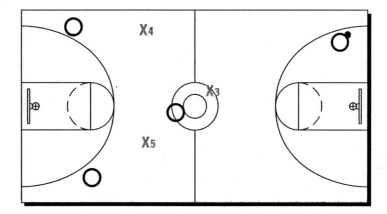

Diagram 17

As you can see in Diagram 17, for the sake of simplicity, we have lined up the offense in a 2-1-2 set. The offense could be 2-1-2 or 1-3-1, for that matter, and the matchup responsibilities would be the same. The back-line people simply match up with an offensive player in their area. In the case of the 2-1-2 or 1-3-1, we will designate who the back man is going to be. In general, we would look at the physical abilities of the X4 and X5 and choose the more mobile of the two to be the deepest defender.

We try to keep the ball from being passed to the middle of the floor. We need to be able to defend a stationary offensive player working the middle of the floor or a man who flashes into the center from behind the defense. No matter how the offensive man gets there, we deny all passes to the middle of the basketball court.

We also deny any pass that would cause us to have to change the ball-side box. The most common passes used by the offense to change sides of the court are the diagonal skip pass or the flatter skip pass. Diagram 18 shows both these types of passes and where the defenders must go to prevent them. We never want the ball passed from one side to the other. There are times that we will force the dribbler to the middle, but never the pass. A pass caught in the middle of the floor by the offense puts all other defenders one pass removed, and we have no designated help.

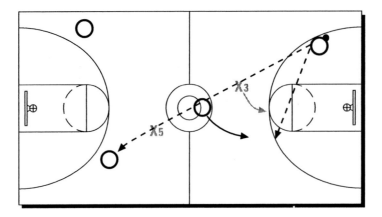

Diagram 18

As we look at the responsibilities of the back three defenders, keep in mind that the smaller we can make the box, the less ground we have to cover in our rotations and slides. By keeping passes from being received in the middle of the court, we keep our offside defenders in a designated help position. Passes that travel across the court cause our bigger players to have to sprint to help. Passes farther into the box not only make the box smaller, but they also shorten our rotations and drops.

SPECIFIC RESPONSIBILITIES OF THE BACK THREE DEFENDERS

X3

- He must prevent the ball from being passed to the middle of the floor against a 2-1-2 alignment.

- He is off toward the ball and in line to discourage dribble penetration to the middle of the floor.

- He stays on the line when off the ball, cutting down the vision of the dribbler coming toward the help-side box.

- If the ball is thrown to the middle of the court, X3 will become the on-the-ball defender and attempt to make sure the offensive player dribbles back to the box from where the ball was passed and/or pass the ball back into the box from where it was passed.

- He never lets the offensive player catch and reverse the ball to the help-side box.

- He never overruns the ball when he tries to make a steal.

X4

- He stays on the line to discourage the ball from being passed directly up the floor. We would rather trap a dribble than a pass.

- He stays on the line so he doesn't have to waste a step getting in the line before he closes to trap the dribbler.

- He stays in a pistols position with his head on a swivel, moving, so he will not lose sight of either the ball or his man.

X5

- He must stay on the line and up the line so he can take away the long diagonal skip pass.

- He is the anchor, the basket protector, the last line of defense for the press.

- He must be able to protect the basket and not give away easy or uncontested shots around the paint area.

Diagram 19 shows the on-the-line, up-the-line positions by the back three defenders as they begin their specific responsibilities.

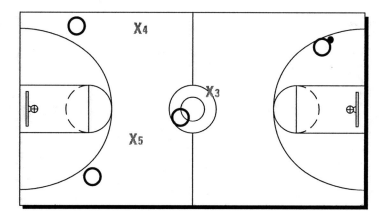

Diagram 19

CHAPTER 6

Rotations and Drops Versus
a Variety of Alignments

Before we get into the main part of this chapter on rotations and drops, here are some keys that we need to stress to the athletes if we are going to successfully press our opposition:

- We can vary our pickup point (see Chapter 9), depending on what we want to accomplish for a specific opponent or at that particular moment in the game.

- The pickup point can be full court, three-quarter court, or half court.

- No matter where we decide to pick up the offense, the basic pressure remains the same.

- There is no way we can determine the setup or positioning of the offensive players.

- The offense will dictate how we line up to match them and how we position our personnel. After that, we attempt to determine the movement and location of the ball by our pressure and influence.

- We want to break down and disrupt their spacing, causing them to throw longer passes than they are used to.

- We encourage their "nonplayers" to make the plays instead of their players, by virtue of where we force the ball and where we allow it to be caught.

- We also accomplish this by trapping the decision-making players, forcing them to get rid of the ball to non–decision-making players.

- We try not to trap the non–decision-makers; instead, we just pressure them and force them to play faster than they are capable.

- The key concept is to trap with two of our players on the ball, two players anticipating the pass and one player protecting the basket. We will discuss in detail the principles of effective trapping in Chapter 7.

ROTATIONS AND COVERAGES IN THE MATCHUP PRESS

In this chapter we will look at some of the possible rotations we would make against a variety of offensive alignments. We cannot cover every offensive possibility, but if our players follow the simple matchup guidelines and play aggressively, they will be fine. Most often, through scouting reports, we will have a good idea about the type of press offense we will face; but even if we do not know ahead of time, we can see early in the contest how a team plans on attacking our pressure and then adjust accordingly. Most teams have one primary method of breaking a press, with possibly a second. Once we have seen what they want to do, it becomes our goal to match up and identify who their decision-makers are and how to get the ball out of their hands and into the hands of the non–decision-makers.

ROTATIONS VS. A 2-1-2 OFFENSE

Diagram 20 illustrates the rotations we make against a 2-1-2 offense, once the ball has been inbounded to O1 and all defenders have matched up. These are the rotations we would make if X4's man is at the foul line extended or above, and we are forcing toward the sideline.

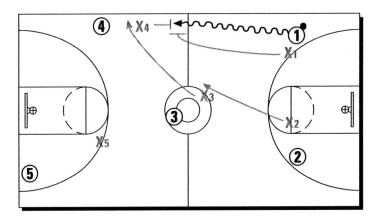

Diagram 20

From Diagram 20, here are the rotations and responsibilities for all five defenders in our matchup press.

X1
- Closes out on the receiver and influences him down the sideline.

- Splits the offensive player in half, keeping half of his body ahead of the ball so that the dribbler cannot turn to the middle of the court.

- Becomes the top man in the trap with X4, once the dribbler has crossed the half-court line.

X4
- He is responsible for the first trap if his offensive matchup is above the foul line extended.

- As he approaches to trap, he must stay directly in the passing lane.

- Attacks the ball with his knees bent and hips down so he can move his feet with the movement of the dribbler.

- As he approaches the trap, he keeps his hands and arms raised to take away the vision of the dribbler.

- He is responsible for cutting off the sideline while working with X1.

X1 and X4
- They are the two players involved in trapping the ball.

- The ideal trap occurs as soon as the offensive dribbler crosses half court.

- The two players trap foot to foot, locking their legs to prevent the offensive player from splitting them.

- Both players need to trap aggressively, with their hips down and their hands up.

- It is extremely important to teach your players that when they trap, they must stay down in their defensive stance and still have their hands raised. The natural tendency is for the players trapping to raise their hips and knees when they raise their hands. It is a biological fact that your hips and hands are not directly connected.

X2
- Rotates to the middle of the floor and finds a man to match up with.

- He must anticipate when and where the ball is going to be thrown.

- He anticipates by reading the shoulders (rather than the eyes) of the man with the ball; the passer will turn his shoulders in the direction he is going to pass.

- If he is in doubt, he always protects from the inside out.

X3

- Rotates to the man X4 leaves and gets in line.

- Looks to make the steal of the pass, coming out of the trap, or simply matches up with the receiver.

- The players rotating can *never* overrun the ball. We believe this is the worst play in basketball and spells disaster for your press.

- If the ball arrives before X3 does, he guards the man head up, influencing him farther into the box.

- He can *never* allow the man to catch the ball and drive to the middle.

- If the offensive man is a non–decision-maker, we may allow him to catch the ball and then try to rush him.

X5

- He is the anchor, and although he is on the line and up the line, his main job is to protect the basket.

- He stays in line with his matchup so they cannot throw a diagonal pass that would make us change boxes.

- Only once in a great while, he can shoot the gap if the offensive man in the middle sinks to the top of the key or below.

Remember: The key is to make the offense look open and then rotate to them. This defense can either help you speed up the pace of the opponent or slow them down, depending on how aggressively or conservatively you wish to play it.

CONTINUATION OF THE ROTATIONS VS. THE 2-1-2—SECOND TRAP

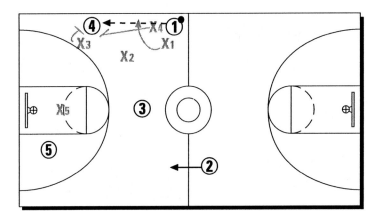

Diagram 21

Diagram 21 shows the defenders' responsibilities after the ball has been passed out of the first trap. We are still forcing to the sideline.

X1
- As the ball is passed out of the trap and farther into the box, he sprints to help, on the line and up the line.

- He denies the ball back to the man who was in the first trap so as to prevent the ball from coming out of the box.

X2
- He drops farther into the middle to locate a new matchup or stay with the same man.

- He denies any pass to the man in the middle.

- He is prepared to drop to the basket if, for some reason, X5 has to vacate that area.

X3
- Controls and contains the ball.

- He is responsible for shutting off the drive to the basket.

- As X4 drops to trap with him, he has the responsibility of not letting the offense dribble out of the trap on the low side.

- He becomes the low man in the trap.

- He attacks with his hands high to affect the vision of the receiver.

X4
- Leaves the trap with X1 and follows the pass down the sideline and stays in line with the man he is leaving.

- As he closes out on the receiver, he contains the offensive player from driving to the middle of the floor.

- Once he is in the trap with X3, he becomes the top man and is responsible for not letting the offensive player out of the trap to the high side.

X5
- Sinks with the pass so he can stay on the line and up the line to prevent any crosscourt skip pass.

- He guards anyone in the lane area around the basket.

- He must communicate to the other defenders about potential receivers, especially to the defender dropping into the high-post area (in this case, X2).

- If there is not an offensive player in the basket or lane area, he takes any cutter to the basket.

- He remains the anchor of the defense, protecting the defense.

CONTINUATION OF THE ROTATIONS VS. A 2-1-2—THIRD TRAP

Diagram 22 shows the responsibilities of the five defenders as the ball gets passed out of the second trap and into the corner to O5, who has circled into the ball-side corner. Notice we are still forcing toward the sideline, and the box is still getting smaller and smaller and the rotations are getting shorter.

Diagram 22

X1
- He sprints to help on the line and up the line versus the man who passed out of the second trap.

- He denies the pass out of the trap and back to the wing, which would enlarge the box.

X2
- He dives in to the high-post area.

- Gets in line with any potential receiver in that area.

- If no one is in the high post, he finds the next closest man to the ball.

- If X4 gets hung up while he is trying to dive to the basket, or if X2 is much closer, he can assume the basket coverage.

- He reads the shoulders of the man in the trap to try to anticipate and steal any pass out of the corner.

X3
- Leaves the second trap and follows the pass while staying in line.

- He contains the receiver from driving to the middle of the floor.

- He becomes the top man in the trap and does not allow the dribbler to get out of the trap on the high side.

X4
- As the ball gets passed out of the trap, he must dive to protect the basket (for rebounding purposes, we cannot have all three big people out on the perimeter of the floor).

- Gets to the basket by making a three-step drop.

- Fronts anyone in the low-post area.

- If, by chance, X2 has dived into the basket area, he must find any unguarded player in the high-post area and deny the ball to him.

- If he is in the low-post instead of X2, he becomes the anchor and must protect the basket.

X5
- Attacks the ball with his hands up and his hips low.

- Contains the receiver in the corner.

- He does not force to the baseline, but rather simply contains the man in the trap.

- He is the low man in the third trap and cannot allow him to get out of the trap on the low side.

ROTATIONS VS. A 2-1-2 SET WHEN X4'S MAN IS BELOW THE FOUL LINE

If the man whom X4 is matched up with is lined up lower than the foul line extended, we will rotate and trap differently. We are still forcing to the sideline and trapping over the half-court line. Diagram 23 shows the rotation we would use in this scenario.

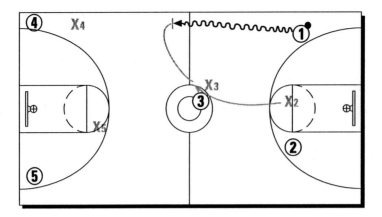

Diagram 23

X1

- He continues to influence the dribbler to the sideline and attempt to keep him there by using the correct footwork and stance on the ball.

- As he crosses half court, X1 will trap with X3.

- All the rest of his rules remain the same from this point on.

X2

- As the ball is being dribbled up the sideline, he stays on the line and up the line to prevent a pass that would reverse the ball out of the box.

- He should be aware of the possibility that X3 may be the one leaving to trap with X1, so he must shade the middle a little bit more than normal.

- He must get to the middle man quicker when X3 leaves to trap and deny any pass to the middle of the floor.

- Once the trap has taken place, X2 must guard the offensive man in the middle of the court.

X3

- Sees that X4 is matched deeper than the foul line extended and knows he has trap responsibilities.

- Leaves the middle to go trap with X1.

- Again, the ideal trapping location is that point at which the dribbler crosses the half-court line.

- He must attack with his hands high to take away vision and his knees bent so he can defend the dribble.

- He becomes the bottom man on the trap and is the defender who follows the next pass to the sideline and becomes the top man on the next trap.

X4

- Communicates to X3 that his man is below the foul line extended.

- Stays in line to prevent a direct pass.

- He prevents the pass because there is no other constructive drop for him to make.

- He needs to be aware if the man he is matched with is a shooter or not (many teams will put their best shooter deep in the corner, outside the three-point line).

X5

- He remains in line in the middle of the floor.

- He must be aware of the middle man dropping to the basket.

- If the man in the middle receives the ball, he retreats to the basket.

- His primary goal remains the same: to be the anchor of the defense and to protect the goal against any easy or unguarded shots.

ROTATIONS VS. THE 2-1-2 PRESS OFFENSE WHEN WE ARE FORCING TO THE MIDDLE

The responsibilities of the defenders change if we are influencing the dribbler to the middle of the court. Diagram 24 shows the rotations of all five defenders when we are forcing to the middle or trying to get the ball handler to use a spin dribble.

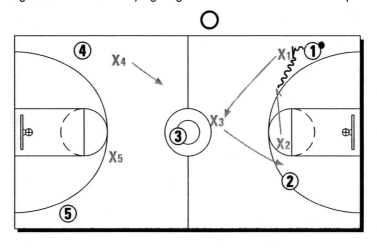

Diagram 24

X1

- As he closes out on the receiver, X1 plays the man more head up rather than playing him a half a man ahead.

- If the dribbler goes to the sideline, he tries to force him to reverse his direction by using a spin dribble.

- If the dribbler spins, X1 anticipates the rotation and help from X2 and X3 and sprints to the middle of the floor and takes X3's man.

- Once he has matched up, he denies the pass to the middle man.

X2

- He must know that we are going to force to the middle and be looking for the spin dribble.

- As soon as the dribbler turns his back and begins to spin to the middle, X2 runs at him.

- As he attacks the dribbler, X2 keeps his hands up to force the lob or bounce pass (both of these type passes take longer to get to their intended receiver).

- Our rule on attacking the ball is that the pass must go over us or under us, but never through us; a direct pass is too quick, and the defense is not able to rotate fast enough to catch up.

- If the offensive man keeps his dribble alive, X2 should attempt to force him back to the side, and we will continue trapping the sideline.

X3

- As X2 leaves, he shoots the gap between the offensive guards, looking for the interception.

- He either steals the pass or defends the offside guard.

- He can never overrun the ball.

- If the ball is forced back to the sideline, he assumes the responsibilities that X2 would normally have.

X4

- He must stay in line and prevent the direct pass.

- He prevents the pass because there is no other constructive drop for him to make.

- He needs to understand the strengths of the man he is guarding, since many teams place their best perimeter shooter in the corner to spot up for a three.

X5

- He remains in the middle of the floor in line.

- Needs to be aware if the middle man drops to the basket.

- If the middle man does receive the ball, he needs to retreat to the basket.

- He remains the anchor and protects the basket as the last line of defense.

ROTATION VS. 2-1-2 WHEN FORCING TO THE MIDDLE (CONTINUED)

Diagram 25 shows the continuation of Diagram 24 if O1 keeps his dribble after the run-and-jump rotation that took place while forcing him to spin. The matchup press goes back to the same principles of trapping the sideline if O1 is forced back to the side.

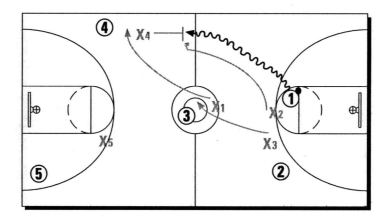

Diagram 25

X1

- Has assumed the job of the middle man, and as the trap is made, he rotates to cover O4.

- Will trap with X4 if the ball is passed down to O4.

X2

- Forces the dribbler back to the sideline and traps with X4, taking the top side of the trap.

- Will sprint to help on a pass down the sideline.

X3

- Comes off from being in line with O2 to take away the direct pass to the middle.

X4

- His man is above the free throw line extended, so he comes up to trap with X1 and takes the bottom side of the trap.

- He will follow the next pass down and be the top man on the next trap.

X5

- Stays in line to prevent the diagonal skip pass and protects the basket.

ROTATIONS VS. A 2-1-2 SET WHEN THE BALL IS REVERSED OUT OF THE TRAP

Diagram 26 shows the rotation out of the trap just over half court if the ball gets reversed back to the guard. The description of responsibilities begins with X3 and X1 trapping O1 because O4 is below the foul line extended, and X2 rotating and covering the offensive player in the middle of the court.

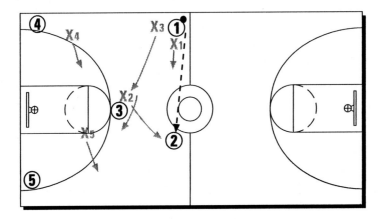

Diagram 26

X1

- Leaves the trap and sprints to help in a position to deny the pass back to the guard (O1), who just reversed the ball.

- We cannot allow the ball to be swung back and forth from guard to guard, making us constantly changing boxes.

X2

- Holds his position on O3 for a count to give X3 time to be on his way to cover the middle man.

- Closes out on O2, who has just received the ball.

- Influences him to the near sideline.

- Anticipates following a pass to the corner and becoming the high-side defender in a trap with X5.

- Always attacks the ball with hands high to disrupt vision and hips and knees bent to be able to defend the live dribble.

X3
- Leaves the trap with X1 while the ball is in the air.

- Sprints in a straight-line drop to cover the middle man.

- Always drops to the ball side of the potential receiver.

- It is useless to drop behind the offensive player and allow him to catch the ball in the middle of the floor.

- Readies himself to drop to X5's man if X5 leaves to trap with X2.

X4

- Goes from on-the-line, up-the-line with O1 to sprint to help position on the line with O2.

- Becomes the anchor on the backside, protecting the basket.

X5
- Sprints in line, up the line with his man.

- Anticipates a trap with X2.

As you can see, we are still in our trap. The only thing that has happened is that the ball was reversed, which changes the box and the ball-side, help-side responsibilities of each defender.

ROTATIONS VS. A 1-3-1 OFFENSIVE SET

Once we have determined how our opponent is going to line up to attack our press, we make the small adjustments necessary to cover their primary alignment. Next, we will explain how we rotate, drop and trap a 1-3-1 alignment. Diagram 27 shows the offense in a 1-3-1 alignment after the ball has been inbounded, as well as how we match up and rotate to cover this set.

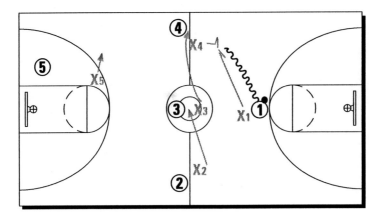

Diagram 27

X1

- Matches up with the point and works to get him out of the middle of the floor.

- He can force the ball to either sideline by splitting the ball handler in half, keeping half of his body ahead of the ball to cut off the middle of the court (in this case, he directs the ball toward X4).

- He will be the top man on a double-team on either side of the floor.

- Once the trap is set, he cannot allow the dribbler to get out of the trap to the middle of the court.

X4

- Attacks the ball with his hands high and knees and hips flexed.

- He is responsible for shutting the dribbler off from sideline penetration (he cannot let him turn the corner).

- Once in the trap, he is the bottom man.

- He needs to be ready to follow the pass and rotate down the sideline to the next trap with X3.

X3

- Makes the diagonal rotation to take away the direct pass to O4.

- Never overruns the ball, which would create an outnumbered situation for the dribbler to attack the basket.

- He shuts off the pass by being in line, looking to make a steal or guard O4, depending on the strengths and weaknesses of the offensive player.

- Never allows the man with the ball to catch and drive to the middle, which would put all four other defenders in a help situation.

X2
- Makes the drop to the middle man and denies.

- Never overruns the ball.

- Dives in front of the middle man—not behind him.

X5
- He remains up the line with his matchup.

- Protects the basket as the last line of defense.

After the first trap, all the other traps follow the same principles we have discussed before. The low man in the trap follows the pass to double-team the receiver. The high man in the trap rotates to shut off the reversal pass out of the new trap. Each time the ball goes farther into the box, each defender rotates and follows the same rules. Diagram 28 shows the rotations of the defenders if 01 passes the ball to 04.

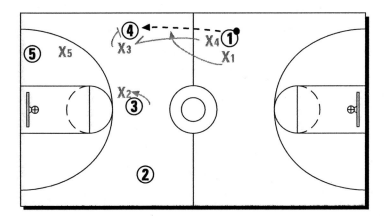

Diagram 28

Diagram 29 illustrates the next pass and trap if the ball goes to 05 in the corner. Again, it is essential that X4 drive hard to the paint to make sure we have basket coverage and at least one big player to rebound.

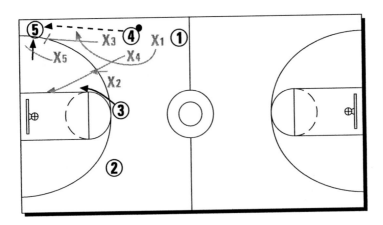

Diagram 29

ROTATIONS VS. A 1-3-1—FORCING TO THE MIDDLE

Diagram 30 illustrates the matchup assignments, rotations, drops and traps if our opponent uses a 1-3-1 alignment to try to break our press, and we are forcing to the middle.

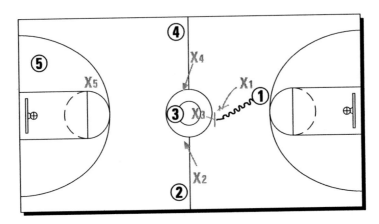

Diagram 30

X1

- Assumes a stance to influence the dribbler to the middle of the floor.

- He attempts to force the dribbler toward X3 without letting the ball handler split the two of them.

- Traps the ball with X3.

- Once in the trap, X1 does not let the dribbler come back to the side he came in from.

- Since he is trapping a live dribble, he must keep very active feet.

X2
- Dives into the middle to split his man and the middle man.

- Anticipates where the pass is going to be thrown and prepares to make the next rotation, depending on where the ball goes.

- He must guard the middle first, since any pass to the middle of the court would take away the establishment of any kind of box.

X3
- As the ball is being forced to the middle, he attacks the ball with his hands high and his hips down.

- Since he is trapping a live dribble, he must keep his feet very active.

- He traps on the side opposite X1.

- He has to be very careful not to allow 01 to split the two of them with the dribble.

- He and X1 take away the center of the floor with their hands so as not to allow a pass to that area of the court.

- He must stay very active and aggressive in the trap.

X4
- Dives to the middle, splitting his man and the middle man.

- He anticipates where the next pass is going to be thrown and prepares to make the next rotation.

- He must defend the middle first and influence the pass to go to the sideline.

X5
- He stays up the line, looking for a run-out by any of the three offensive players in the half court.

- Protects the basket as the anchor of the defense.

CONTINUED ROTATION VS. A 1-3-1 OFFENSIVE SET WHEN FORCING TO THE MIDDLE

Once we have trapped the ball in the middle of the court with X1 and X3, we want to force the pass out of the trap to be thrown to the sideline. From there, all the rotations remain the same as described before. The low man in the trap follows the ball to trap again; the high man from the trap shuts off the reversal; and all other rotations follow the same principles of the matchup.

Diagram 31 is an example of the rotations after X1 and X3 have forced the pass to be thrown to the sideline to O2.

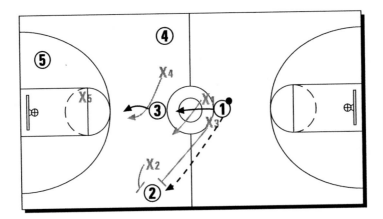

Diagram 31

X1

- Drops out of the trap to deny any potential ball reversal to O1, who must cross the center line.

- He gets on the line with the ball and O1 as O1 moves into the frontcourt.

X2

- Moves from his position of protecting the middle to closing out on the receiver.

- As he closes out, he forces to the sideline to decrease the size of the box.

- He anticipates the arrival of X3, who will help him trap O2.

- Once in the trap, he must eliminate the possibility of O2 splitting the trap or going baseline.

- As the bottom man in the trap, he must prepare to follow, and trap any pass that goes deeper into the corner.

X3

- Dives out of the trap with X1 to follow the pass and trap with X2 on the sideline.

- He becomes the top defender in the trap who must take away O2's ability to dribble out of the trap, over the top.

- If O2 passes the ball farther into the corner, he denies the reversal back to O2.

- He must trap with active feet, since he is trapping a live dribble.

X4
- Rotates from the middle of O4 and O3 to the ball side of O3 and gets there while the ball is in the air.

- He denies any direct pass to the middle and prepares to drop farther toward the basket if O3 slides to that area.

- He leaves O4 open as the man farthest from the ball.

X5
- He continues to move as the ball is passed, in order to stay on the line and up the line to deny any direct diagonal pass.

- Covers O5 if he moves to the ball-side corner and communicates that he is leaving the basket area.

- If O5 does not move to the corner, he remains as the basket protector.

ROTATIONS VS. A 2-2-1 OFFENSIVE SET

If the offensive strategy to attack the press includes a 2-2-1 set, we would match up and play against this alignment as if we are in a 2-2-1 press. After the ball has been inbounded and they get into their set, we will follow the same principles as before. Diagram 32 illustrates the rotations, drops and traps we would utilize against this offensive set, if we were trying to force the ball to the sideline.

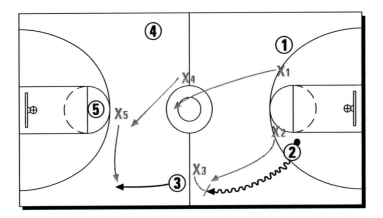

Diagram 32

X2
- If the ball is inbounded to O2, X2 would close out and influence with his stance to force the ball to the sideline.

- He traps with X3 and becomes the top man in the trap, assuming all the responsibilities that come with that spot.

X3
- Starts on the line, up the line with O3 to deny any direct pass.

- Comes up to trap with high hands to take away vision.

- He is responsible in the trap for shutting off the sideline.

- He must keep his feet active to trap a live dribbler.

- He is the low man in the trap and must prepare to follow and trap any pass that goes deeper into the corner.

X4
- Starts and stays on the line and up the line with O4, as O2 dribbles the ball down the sideline.

- As the trap is made, he sees O5 leave the basket area to cover O3, and he sprints to X5's man.

- He gets on a line between the ball and the potential receiver in the basket area.

- If he is too slow in his rotation, he will give up an easy basket.

- Once established in the anchor position, he protects the basket, as X5 had done.

X5

- Starts in the anchor position and protects the basket.

- As the ball is being dribbled down the sideline and into the trap, he must watch for any of the offensive players on his side being left open on a rotation.

- In this case, O3 moves down the sideline, so X5 rotates to him.

- As he vacates the basket area, he must communicate with the help-side defenders (X4) to take his coverage in the back of the press.

- In covering O3, he cannot overrun the ball.

- He stays in line to take away a direct pass and prepares to trap if the pass is completed to O3.

X1

- Dives from his original position to the middle of the floor.

- Has to look to find a man to match up with.

- In this case, he matches with O4.

- He works to keep the ball in the sideline box by denying any reversal.

ROTATIONS VS. A 2-2-1 SET (WEAKSIDE FLASH)

One of the most common methods of breaking a press is to flash a receiver into the middle of the court from the weak side. This maneuver is something we will usually have to defend in a 2-2-1 set. Diagram 33 shows the rotations we would make to stop this strategy. The diagram illustrates where our defenders would be after the ball has been inbounded.

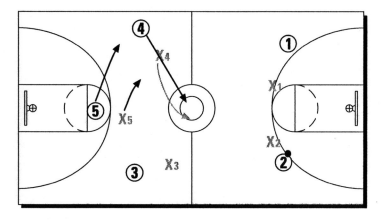

Diagram 33

X4

- Simply stays with his matchup and denies the flash, beating the man to the spot in the middle of the floor.

- He should verbalize to his teammates that there is a cutter to the middle, since it changes their responsibilities.

- He then assumes the same responsibilities he would have in defending a 2-1-2 set.

X1, X2, X3, X5

- They should see and hear when X4 covers the flash to the middle from the weak side.

- They play it as they would in our 2-1-2 press.

- Remember that most teams will only throw the ball to the sideline so they can throw it back to the middle for the primary attack.

- Very few teams have a press attack that uses the sideline exclusively.

ROTATIONS VS. 2-2-1 SET (CURL ON THE BALL SIDE)

One of the techniques that our opponents will use to attempt to break our press is what we call "curling the ball-side man." In this case, the player down the floor from the ball will curl into the middle of the floor as the dribbler approaches him. This creates some different rotations for the ball-side defender (X4). Diagram 34 illustrates the curl on the ball side and the rotations we use to combat this maneuver.

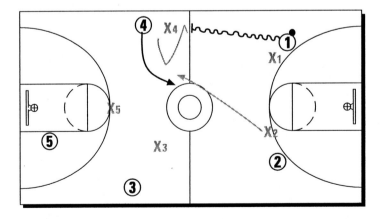

Diagram 34

X1

- Forces the ball to the sideline and attempts to keep it there.

- He splits the offensive player in half, keeping his body ahead of the ball so he will not get cut back to the middle of the court.

- He will become the top man on the trap with X4 and assume the responsibilities of that position.

X2

- Stays on the line, up the line as the ball is being dribbled down the sideline.

- As the trap occurs, he drops to the middle of the floor.

- He takes O4, who has curled into the center of the court.

- As he cuts to cover O4, he must dive in front of him—not behind him.

- He denies the ball being caught in the middle of the floor.

- He cannot overrun the ball and let the middle man go on the attack.

X3

- He stays on the line and up the line.

- He looks for O4 trying to release to the foul line area, in which case he needs to help in that area.

- He will take O4 if he releases to the basket, because X2 would have to drop way too far.

X4

- Leads his man to the middle on the curl.

- He cannot let O4 catch the ball in the middle.

- As X2 drops to cover O4, he rotates to the sideline to trap with X1.

- In the trap, he is the low man responsible for stopping sideline penetration and attacking with high hands.

- Prepares to drop to the next trap if the ball is passed down the sideline.

X5

- Protects the basket.

- Stays in line with his matchup so as not to allow a diagonal pass.

- Must be ready to help on a basket cut by O4.

- Needs to be the voice of the press so that all other defenders can be made aware of player movement behind them.

ROTATIONS VS. 2-2-1 SET (BALL-SIDE CURL AND BACKSIDE FILL)

Another technique teams use against our press is curling a receiver on the ball side to the middle and then filling his spot from the backside. Diagram 35 shows the rotations we would use in this case.

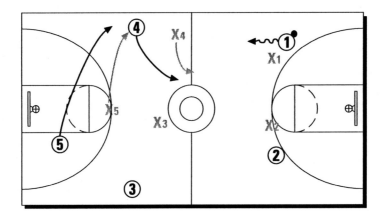

Diagram 35

X4
- Leads his man into the middle as he curls.

- Denies him the direct pass.

- When he hears X5 leave the basket to cover the backside cutter on the sideline, he assumes the same responsibilities as our 2-1-2 press.

X5
- Leads his man to the ball on the backside cut and calls out to X4 where he is going.

- Stays on the line, up the line.

- He must be ready to come up and trap with X1, as he would in the 2-1-2 press.

X1, X2, X3
- Assume the same responsibilities they would have versus a 2-1-2 offensive scheme.

CHAPTER 7

Effective Trapping

Trapping is an essential ingredient in our defensive scheme. Whether it is in half court or full court, we depend on being able to successfully trap the ball handler. Once we have trapped the ball, we need to be able to follow up with correct rotations by our other three defenders. We can rotate to positions on the floor, where we can either attempt to intercept the next pass or at least dictate who can catch the ball or which part of the floor is going to be open.

Because trapping is so critical to our defensive principles, it is extremely important that our players are well skilled in the techniques necessary to trap. The method we teach for trapping is the same, whether it is done in our man-to-man zone or matchup. Although the actual trap only involves two defenders, the whole team has to understand and execute the concepts in order for us to win this phase of the game.

In simplest terms, trapping is just going from one-on-one defense to a situation where two defenders attack the ball handler, while the remaining three immediately move into a zone coverage.

A good trap is when two players surround the offensive player with their feet together, or, better yet, with their legs locked. We tell our players that it is the responsibility of the second defender to the trap to lock (overlap) their legs. This prevents the offensive player from splitting the trap. Depending on their position, one trapper takes away the outside or sideline drive, and the other takes away the split, as well as preventing any reverse dribble that would allow penetration to the middle of the court. As we approach the trap, both players need to work together to influence the ball handler where they want him to go. The second man coming into the trap uses the last two steps to control his speed and slide into the trap, staying low and maintaining a good defensive stance. He needs to be aware of his responsibility, either sideline or middle.

Next, we want to take away space in the trap. The defenders have as much right to the unclaimed space as the offense does. This is the rule of verticality, which is often not interpreted correctly by officials. We want our players in the trap to concentrate on keeping their knees bent and their hips down, especially if the person we are trapping has his dribble alive. A defender who is standing straight up cannot stop a live dribbler, and then we will end up chasing instead of containing.

We want our players in the trap to get there quickly and have their arms and hands straight up in the air. To overteach this point, we ask them to get their elbows behind their ears. This action gets their hands and arms back so that they are not tempted to reach. We do not want to bail out the player who is trapped by fouling him. Once the dribble has been terminated, we can close out harder with our hands and "trace," or "point," the ball (i.e., make a mirror-like movement), following the ball with both hands, wherever it moves. The purpose is to take away vision and any direct pass. The only passes we want to allow the offensive player to throw out of the trap are a bounce or a lob, both of which take time to arrive, thus giving us a chance to rotate or intercept.

ANTICIPATING THE PASS OUT OF THE TRAP

I have heard many coaches tell their players to "read the passer's eyes." Most of my players don't have good enough eyesight to see someone's eyes from 15 to 20 feet away. Besides, I am always wary of those tricky eyes. We found it to be more predictable and easier to read the offensive man's shoulders. Think about how hard it is to throw out of a trap without pointing your shoulders at the target. Diagram 36 illustrates the theory of "reading the shoulders."

Diagram 36

In order for O1 to throw a pass to O2, O3 or O4, he must give his pass away by turning his shoulders and facing his target in order to get any power on his pass. This small move will allow our defenders off the trap to anticipate the direction the pass is going to come out of the trap and rotate correctly.

Most offensive teams are coached to give the man in the trap at least three potential passing outlets:

1. *Directly in Line.* This is the first look for the man with the ball. As the dribbler is bringing the ball down the court and sees the trap coming, he looks straight ahead first. If he is being influenced to the sideline, he will be protecting the ball and have, in this case, his left shoulder forward. In some cases, his shoulders could be parallel to the half-court line. Either way, this positioning makes it very difficult, if not impossible, for him to pass to O2 (the trailing guard) at half court. This tells us we should anticipate potential passes to O3 or O4 with the players not involved in the trap.

2. *The Middle Man.* In order to make this pass, the offensive man with the ball must turn his left shoulder in the direction of the target. This move puts the offensive man in more of an open position. When this happens, it tells our two anticipators to head in the other direction, cheating more toward the half-court area.

3. *Passing to the Trailer.* For the offensive man in the trap to pass out of effective trap to the trailer at half court (O2), he must almost totally open up with his shoulders perpendicular to the half-court line. This action would be a signal for our two anticipators to cover the middle and the trailer (O3 and O2). The only other way an offensive player could pass to O2 would be by totally turning his back to O4 and O3 and point his right shoulder toward the target. This means our two anticipators are covering the O3 and O2 like a blanket. They may also choose to make it appear to be open and cut in front for the steal.

The key concept for the trapping team is to trap with two players on the ball, two players anticipating the pass and one player protecting the basket area. When in doubt, the anticipators must cover people from the inside out. Shortening the box will not consistently beat you, but allowing the ball to get to the middle of the floor gives the offensive team a tremendous advantage.

Diagrams 37 and 38 show the principle of having two on the ball (X), two as anticipators (A) and one player protecting the goal (P).

KEYS TO TRAPPING

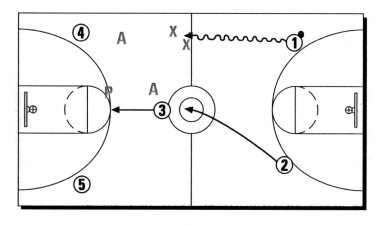

Diagram 37

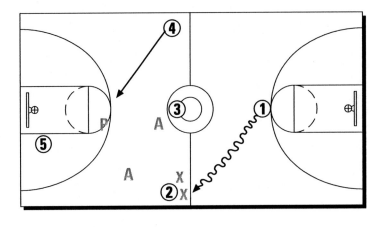

Diagram 38

- Each player must see the big picture and understand where, when and who we want to trap.

- Influence the ball handler to steer him into the best trap locations.

- The second defender to the trap attacks with hands high, knees bent and hips down to contain the dribbler and take away his vision.

- The second player to the trap locks legs to prevent any split.

- Take up space and trace the ball without reaching or fouling.

- Stay in your defensive stance and do not permit the dribbler to escape to either side.

- Guard against allowing any direct passes and encourage a bounce pass or a lob.

- Anticipators read the passer's shoulders and rotate to cover potential receivers.

- Any pass that leaves the trap requires that the two trappers sprint out of the trap and to their new responsibilities.

- Every trap should have two trappers, two anticipators and one player protecting the basket.

- When in doubt, you must cover people from the inside out.

- Attempt to keep the ball in an ever-shortening box and out of the middle of the floor.

- Be ready to go from one trap to the next, identifying what your new responsibility is going to be.

CHAPTER 8

Drills for Individual Pressing Defense

In this chapter, we describe a few of the drills we will use to teach the concepts of staying on the line and up the line in order to be correctly positioned. Diagram 39 starts with the player in an on-the-line, up-the-line position. The coach has the ball, and he moves with the ball, while the offensive player being checked remains stationary. The defense must constantly adjust to the movement of the ball and stay on line.

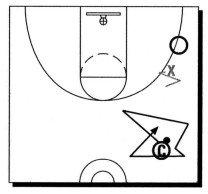

Diagram 39

Diagram 40 shows the same technique with additional players and in full court. You can place all of your players at various places on the court to allow them to make the necessary adjustments to stay on the line.

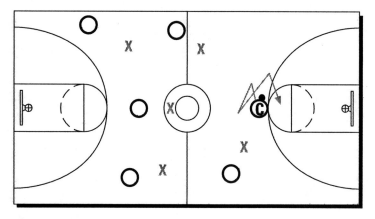

Diagram 40

Diagram 41 illustrates the drill we use to teach the technique with the offensive man moving and the ball staying stationary. Start the defensive player in an on-the-line, up-the-line position. The coach has the ball and remains stationary. The offensive player moves without the ball both vertically and horizontally, while the defender adjusts to stay on the line and works so he can see both the ball and his man.

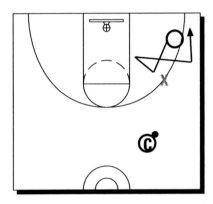

Diagram 41

Once they understand the concept in the individual drill, we move to the team drill, using the full court. Offensive players can move within reasonable boundaries to challenge their defender to stay on the line and up the line and maintain their vision of the man and the ball. Diagram 42 shows this drill on the larger court area.

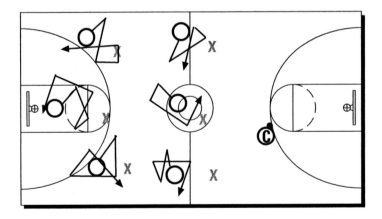

Diagram 42

The third phase of this drill is to have both the ball and the offensive player moving at the same time, while the defender stays on the line and up the line, keeping his vision focused on both the man and the ball. Diagram 43 shows how we introduce this concept one player at a time in the half court.

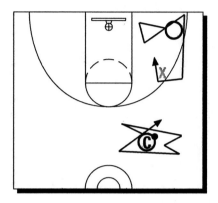

Diagram 43

Diagram 44 shows the same drill done with the whole team at once using the full court. The offensive players can help their partner by working him hard within a limited area and calling out to him if he has lost vision. We use this drill in short bursts and demand maximum effort to perfect this skill.

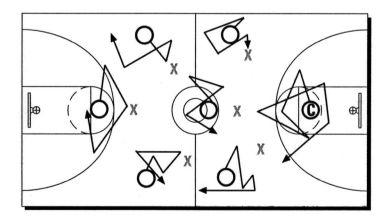

Diagram 44

DRILLS TO TEACH SPRINT TO HELP

The ability of our players to *sprint to help* is key to the success of the overall defense. Although we always attempt to keep the ball on one side of the floor, and within a continually shortening box, there are times when the ball gets reversed and our defenders must be able to react instinctually to adjust to the new box. This is where our sprint-to-help drills have been helpful. The natural tendency of almost any player when the ball is swung away from him is to either relax or drop more toward the basket than to the ball. We spend a lot of time throughout the season teaching our players to *sprint to help* when the ball is reversed from one side of the floor to the other. The goal of the defender is to get to the correct position, on the line and up the line, as quickly as possible when this happens.

A great drill for teaching the mechanics of this skill is illustrated in Diagram 45. It shows the defender on the line and up the line with his matchup to begin the drill.

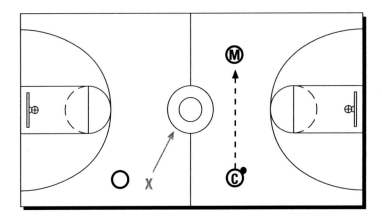

Diagram 45

- The coach starts with the ball and reverses the ball to another coach or manager in the opposite box.

- The defender must then sprint to the middle of the court, readjusting his position to be on the line and up the line within one big step of the newly established box, in a pistols position.

- He attempts to get to that new position as the ball is in the air, so that he is in the proper place when the ball is caught, able to help and able to deny a direct pass to his matchup.

TWO-ON-TWO SPRINT TO HELP

Diagram 46 shows the next drill we work on to teach *sprint to help.*

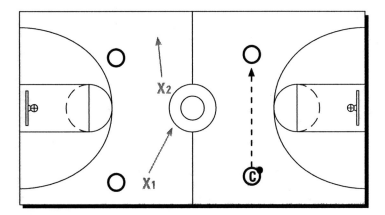

Diagram 46

- X1 is matched with the offensive player in the ball-side box and is on the line and up the line.

- X2 is guarding the man in the help-side box and is on the line and up the line to the ball.

- As the coach reverses the ball, both players sprint to help, getting to their new positions as quickly as possible.

- X1 is now responsible for being within one big step of the new box, and X2 is on the line and up the line, denying any direct pass down the sideline.

- We can swing the ball several times if we want them to make a series of adjustments using the correct techniques.

FOUR-ON-FOUR SPRINT TO HELP

We will increase the number of players working on the skill after they have proven that they understand the concept of sprint to help in the one-on-one and two-on-two drills. The principles are the same, except we have more players on the court at one time, and they are in a variety of positions. At this point, we will have two extra players or managers pass the ball while the coaches stand behind the players who are shifting so the coaches are better able to see and correct individual movement. As coaches, we also attempt to call out the name of the player who is the quickest to move during his adjustment to a new spot.

Diagram 47 illustrates one example of placement of players in the four-on-four sprint-to-help drill. We would work on the shifting against the alignment that we expect the next opponent to be using, so that our practice time and preparation is more specific and beneficial.

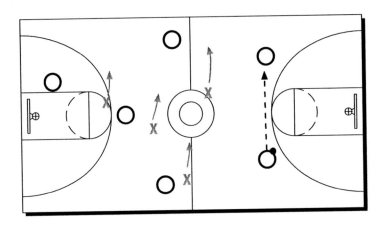

Diagram 47

RUN-AND-JUMP DRILLS

As we discussed in the chapter on rotations, there are times when we force the ball to the middle of the floor or attempt to make the ball handler spin back to the middle of the floor. In these instances, we use a *run-and-jump technique* to defend the middle of the court. The run-and-jump is more of a rotating man-to-man defense using our matchup zone principles. Diagram 48 shows a situation where we would use this technique. This is a predetermined strategy based upon the people we are playing and where we are attempting to influence the ball.

X1 forces the dribbler into a spin dribble back to the center of the court, while X2 and X3 are in the on-the-line and up-the-line positions. As O1 spins back to the middle of the court, X1 stays with him and X2 attacks him with hands high. The natural tendency of most offensive players is to pick up their dribble, which plays right into the hands of the press. As X2 takes his man, X1 rotates back and matches with O3. As X2 leaves to take on the dribbler, X3 holds briefly to keep the ball out of the middle and make it appear that the crosscourt pass to O2 is open. He then rotates up into the passing lane between O1 and O2, making sure that he doesn't overrun the ball, but looking for the deflection or steal.

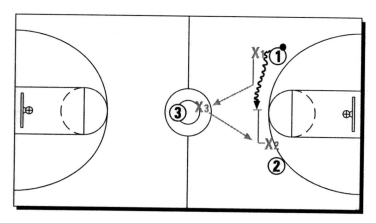

Diagram 48

ONE-ON-ONE—FORCE THE SPIN DRIBBLE

In this drill, we want our defenders who will be matched up with our opponent's guards to be able to influence the dribbler to make a spin dribble. The defensive guard initially influences the ball handler to the sideline and then moves his feet to a position where he is half a man ahead of the dribbler, to force him to turn back to the middle. The defender cannot overrun the ball handler so much that he won't be able to recover in time to control him as he changes direction. He wants the dribbler to turn his back and take the ball to the middle of the floor, still going almost parallel to the half-court line. We will use both sides of the court for this drill and make sure that our defenders can accomplish this skill on either side. We will ask our dribblers to spin back to the middle if the defender has cut off the sideline. Diagram 49 illustrates this drill.

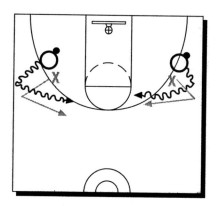

Diagram 49

TWO-ON-TWO RUN-AND-JUMP

Now, we simply add the defender who is going to jump the ball handler as he turns to back into the center of the court. As he turns to come toward the middle, X2 suddenly leaves his man and jumps the dribbler, attempting to surprise him. He attacks with his hands high to take away vision and to prevent a quick pass to O2. When he jumps the dribbler, X2 is looking for a charge if the offensive man is out of control and going too

fast. In game situations, oftentimes the dribbler (if surprised) will travel, pick up the ball or throw a wild pass in the direction the help came from. Any of these choices is an advantage to the defense. X1, who is checking the ball, will release downcourt and look for a new matchup as X2 attacks the dribbler. We will have a coach stand near the center of the court for X1 to locate and match up with. As the defenders become more skilled, we will have the coach move so that the player dropping off the dribbler has to search to match up. He cannot leave too soon and open up an opportunity for the dribbler to split them and head upcourt. Diagram 50 illustrates this drill.

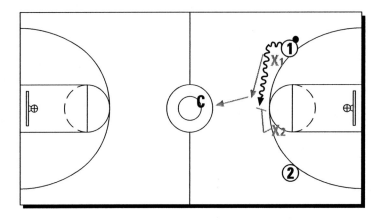

Diagram 50

THREE-ON-THREE RUN-AND-JUMP ROTATION

We will practice this technique from both sides of the floor. In diagram 51, we show the three-on-three drill and rotations.

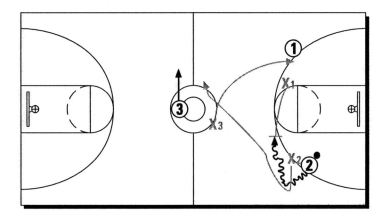

Diagram 51

X2
- Starts on the ball, influencing toward the sideline, and then cuts the dribbler off and forces him back to the middle, hopefully making him use a spin dribble so that he momentarily loses vision and will be more surprised by the defender jumping him.

- As the dribbler turns back to the middle, X2 attempts to "flatten him out," keeping him parallel to the half-court line.

- As X1 begins to jump the dribbler, X2 makes sure to close the gap and not let the dribbler split them; he then releases downcourt to find his next matchup.

- In this case, we are having O3 move to a new location so that X2 has to find him and get on the line and up the line, denying any direct pass.

X1
- Starts on the line and up the line toward O2.

- As the dribbler spins back to the middle of the floor, X1 attacks the ball with hands high to take away the direct pass to O1.

- X1 needs to be able to get to the attack point in a few quick steps.

- If he can time his approach to coincide with the ball leaving the dribbler's hand and going down to the floor, there is a better chance that he will arrive when the ball is not actually in the dribbler's hand, thus forcing the ball handler to pick up the dribble. If the ball is already in the dribbler's hand as X1 attacks, there is a better chance that the offensive man will be able to make a successful pass.

- After he has made the jump, X1 stays with the handler and forces him back to the sideline if his dribble is still alive.

X3

- Reads the run-and-jump situation as soon as the dribbler begins his spin dribble back to the center of the court.

- He needs to time his rotation so he doesn't leave so soon that he allows an opening for the ball handler to make a pass to the man he is leaving.

- As X2 begins his rotation back to the middle, X3 rotates up into the passing lane between O2 and O1.

- He can "bait" the pass by making it look like it is open and then shooting the gap and going for the steal.

- Or he can just deny the pass by getting on the line and up the line.

- Either way, he cannot overrun the ball and allow the offense to head up the court with a numerical advantage.

We will practice these drills on the areas of the court that we anticipate our opponents to align themselves. We will use the run-and-jump tactics against teams whose guards we can out-quick—whose guards are not great ball handlers or decision makers. Another time we will implement the run-and-jump techniques is when we are attempting to get the ball out of the hands of a great individual player. By jumping him, we usually force the ball out of his hands, and then we work hard not to allow the ball to come back to him. Teams that set a ball screen for their guards to break the press are also vulnerable to the run-and-jump.

Even if we do not get a steal, a charge or a travel out of the run-and-jump—and all we end up with is having the defenders switch matchups—we will consider it a successful press if we have not given up a pass or a dribble to the middle of the floor and have kept the ball pinned on the sideline.

If we can keep the ball on the sideline and continually shorten the box, we will look for the sideline traps and rotations described in previous chapters.

DRILLS TO PRACTICE TRAPPING

We need to have our defenders prepared to make effective traps in all areas of the court where we are attempting to influence the ball. We need to be able to trap at half court along the sideline, in the middle if we are facing a 1-3-1 and forcing middle or deep in the corners of the offensive half court. Trapping is a skill that is often overlooked when identifying drills that need to be practiced on a consistent basis.

The following fundamentals need to be separated into specific drills and practiced until they can be accomplished at game speed:

- Anticipating the trap

- Attacking the dribbler

- Trapping a live dribble and keeping it contained

- Trapping a dead dribble

- Rotating out of a trap

In the next few pages, we will describe some of the drills we use to teach these trapping principles. You need to identify the types of traps that you want to execute and then build drills that rehearse those skills.

ANTICIPATING THE TRAP

This drill needs to be done in all the areas of the court where you may be trapping in your defensive system. In Diagram 52, we show how we work with the defender having to anticipate the trap. X4 is on the line and up the line, as X1 forces the ball up the sideline. X4 has to decide if it is a good opportunity to trap on the basis of the speed, vision, spacing and location of the ball. As the ball approaches, he simply calls, "Now!" when he decides to leave his man and attack the ball. While the ball is on the way down the floor, he works on staying on the line and up the line with O4, adjusting each time the ball moves. X4 is looking for a time when he can get to the ball in three quick steps, hopefully just over the half-court line, and not be split. All we are trying to accomplish is to get the trapper to declare when he thinks he has a good trap opportunity and when he would go. This drill can be done in several locations on the floor at a time so that we are getting lots of repetitions.

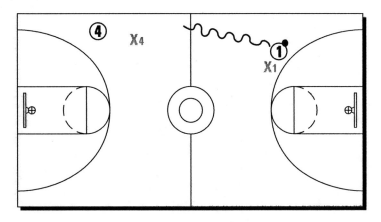

Diagram 52

ATTACKING THE DRIBBLER

Next, we work on the actual attack of the dribbler. Again, it is important to identify all the areas of the court where you want to set your traps in your defensive scheme and then set up a drill that is effective for trapping that area. Diagram 53 shows a drill we use to attack the dribbler at half court when we are forcing to the sideline.

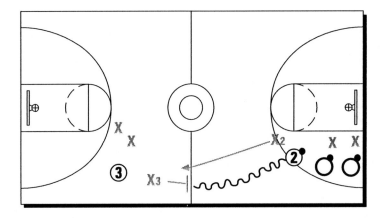

Diagram 53

- X3 works on approaching the dribbler at the correct time and speed so that the two defenders can't be split.

- He must be able to contain the dribbler within the trap.

- The last two steps by X3 are sliding steps, staying low and maintaining a good defensive stance, focusing on his low hips and his high hands as he obstruct vision.

- X3 has to be aware of his sideline containment responsibilities as long as the dribble is still alive.

- The remaining players are waiting at the place where they will be defensively or using the other side of the court

TRAPPING A LIVE DRIBBLE

Often, there are times when we are trapping a ball handler who has not yet dribbled. In these instances, both defenders in the trap have to be skilled in their defensive footwork in order to keep the dribbler contained in the area of the floor where he is trapped. Diagram 54 shows how we work on being in a trap with a ball handler who still has his dribble.

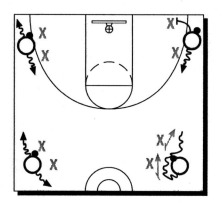

Diagram 54

- Both defenders must maintain their defensive stance, prepared to slide to cover their areas of responsibility, maintaining the correct amount of space and still challenging the vision of the ball handler

TRAPPING THE DEAD DRIBBLE

If the trap involves a ball handler who has picked up his dribble, the defenders can close the amount of space they are trying to occupy and work on mirroring the movement of the ball by tracing it with their hands. We would use the same areas of the floor as in Diagram 54, but this time declare that the dribble is dead and have the defenders work on these skills without fouling. When the dribbler is solidly trapped, we cannot bail him out by fouling him. Remember our goals:

- Get the ball handler to turn his back.

- Hopefully make him throw either a weak bounce pass or a lob out of the trap and into an area of the court that we choose.

- Allow our anticipators to be able to read his shoulders and rotate into the passing lanes.

- Crowd him and trace the ball without fouling.

ROTATING OUT OF THE TRAP

Diagram 55 shows a drill we use to practice the rotation out of one trap and into another. Identify where and how you expect your trappers to be in this situation and then devise drills to use the correct technique and location on the court. Our press provides a lot of opportunities to trap along the sideline and then rotate down the sideline to a second trap, so we use this drill to rehearse that action.

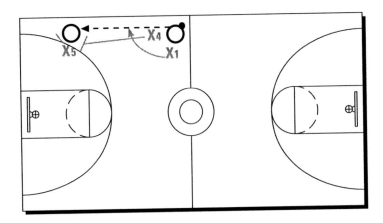

Diagram 55

The drill in Diagram 55 starts with X1 and X4 already in a dead dribble trap.

- X1 and X4 are practicing the techniques involved in trapping and tracing the dead dribbler.

- The player in the trap (it can be a coach) works the trappers before he passes by moving the ball up and down, which causes them to trace it as it moves, and making sure he is not fouled.

- X5 allows the pass down the floor.

- As the ball goes down to the corner, shortening the box, X1 sprints to an on-the-line, up-the-line position so as not to allow the reversal pass back to the man who was just trapped.

- X4 follows the pass into the corner and becomes the top man in a live dribble trap with X5.

- X4 cannot allow the trap to be split or the dribbler to escape over the top to the middle of the floor.

- X5 closes out on the low side, anticipating the trap with X4.

- X5 is responsible for the low side of the trap and cannot allow the dribbler to either split the trap or escape out of the bottom of the trap.

- Both X4 and X5 are working on the techniques involved in trapping a live dribble.

DRILL COMBINING THE SKILLS INVOLVED IN TRAPPING

As soon as our players can anticipate and attack into a trap, trap a live dribble and a dead dribble and rotate out of the trap, we begin to introduce drills that combine the skills and are more game-like. We devise these drills by taking the press and breaking it down into sections. Diagram 56 illustrates an example of a drill that combines influencing the dribbler, trapping, rotation by the ball-side defenders and rotation by the help-side defenders. These are practice situations set up to duplicate what we think we will see from our next opponent and are practiced first at a slower pace to ensure that the rotations are correct and understood. Once the drill is explained and done at a speed to make sure the "defense wins," the offense is allowed to try to defeat the press, and the defenders are expected to execute at game speed.

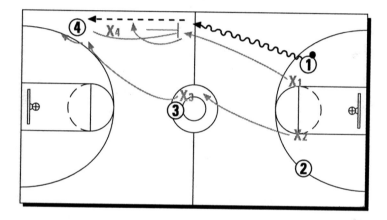

Diagram 56

X1

- Influences the dribbler to the sideline and keeps him there.

- Anticipates the trap coming from X4 and seals the top half of the dead dribble trap.

- Traces the ball and occupies space to control the areas of the floor where 01 can pass the ball.

- As the ball is passed down the floor to the sideline, X1 sprints to a position on the line to prevent a reversal pass.

X2

- Starts on the line and up the line to prevent the ball from changing sides of the court to 02.

- Stays on the line with the ball as it advances into the trap.

- Rotates to take O3 as X3 leaves.

- Rotates to the denial position of O3 as the ball is passed to O4.

X3

- On the line and up the line with O3.

- Anticipates the trap and rotates down to cover O4.

- We practice having X3 take the direct pass away and also having him allow the pass so he can do both on the basis of who and where we are trying to influence the ball.

- He becomes the bottom man in the second trap and assumes those responsibilities.

X4

- Starts on the line and up the line with O4.

- Anticipates the trap.

- Attacks the dribbler at the correct time and uses the correct technique.

- Assumes the responsibilities of the bottom man in the dead-ball trap with X1.

- Dives out of the trap as the ball is passed to the corner and assumes the responsibilities of the top man in a live dribble trap with X5.

SAME MULTIPLE-SKILL DRILL WITH A BALL REVERSAL)

We will use the same setup described in Diagram 56, but then add a ball reversal so that the ball-side and help-side responsibilities are reversed. The drill starts with the ball in O1's hands. After he has taken a dribble or two, we will call "reverse." At this point, we will allow a ball reversal back to O2 and then practice the traps and rotations from this side of the court. As the ball gets swung, O3 moves to the ball side and O4 flashes into the middle of the court.

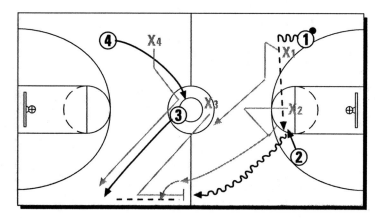

Diagram 57

X1

- Influences O1 to the sideline.

- As the ball is reversed, he jumps to an on-the-line, up-the-line position with O1.

- He moves in line as the ball is dribbled toward half court and then anticipates the trap and rotates to cover the middle man (i.e., O4, who has just flashed into the middle).

- He continues to rotate to stay on line with the second trap and anticipates the pass out.

X2

- Starts on the line with the ball, and then, on the coach's call of "reverse," he allows the ball to be swung to O2.

- He closes out on O2 and influences to the sideline, keeping him pinned.

- He anticipates the trap with X3 and assumes the responsibilities of the top man in a dead-ball trap.

- As the ball is passed down the sideline, he sprints to an on-the-line position to deny the ball back to O2.

X3

- Starts on the line in the middle of the floor.

- As the ball is swung, he adjusts his position and then slides down with O3 to a sideline on-the-line, up-the-line position.

- Anticipates the potential trap with X2 and attacks as the ball crosses half court; also assumes the responsibilities of the bottom man in a dead-ball trap.

- As the ball gets passed down the sideline, he dives into the second trap and assumes the responsibilities of the top man in a live-ball trap with X4.

X4
- Starts on the line and adjusts to the help side on the line as the ball is swung.

- Cuts the flash to the middle and then slides down to cover O3 as X3 traps at half court.

- Assumes the bottom man's role in the second trap with X3.

SCRAMBLE DRILL—4-ON-4 PLUS 1

This is an effective drill we use to help our players learn how to scramble and get to the ball. The defense has one less player than the offense, forcing the defensive players to really move to get the ball covered. This is the same situation every time there is a trap, since we have two people on the ball and are always one player short with the players out of the trap. Our goal in this drill is to get one player on the ball and have two players anticipating and one protecting the basket.

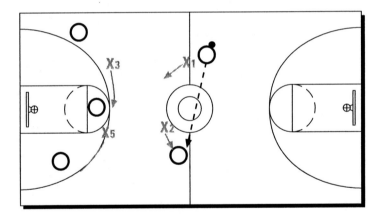

Diagram 58

We play from this setup until the offense scores or the defense gets a stop. We will continue until the defensive team gets three total stops. During the drill, when the offensive team gets an offensive rebound, it will not count as a stop, no matter what happens for the remainder of the play. We do this to emphasize the importance of blocking out, even when we are outnumbered. The defensive players blocking out have to scramble to find an offensive player to get on their back.

CHAPTER 9

Varying the Pressure Points:
Half, Three Quarter and Full Court

Most of our presses that have been described so far are run from three-quarter-court pressure. We can begin our press at almost any area of the court and follow almost the same exact principles. We have found that the same press that may be ineffective at one level of pressure may be completely effective when we move it to another pressure point. For example, we have often started the game in a three-quarter press and not had much success, but by simply adjusting the same defense to either full court or half court, our opponent may really struggle. In general, the quicker we are than our opponent, the more of the court we can defend; the quicker our opponent is compared to us, the less floor space we can successfully defend.

The timing of the press will vary as the level of engagement changes, so you need to practice each press at each level to let your players experience the differences. The smaller the area of the court you are trying to defend, the less you have to worry about matching up and the more you can concentrate on trapping. If you are able to keep the rotations and traps the same from one level of pressure to another, you can really have three defenses in one and not have to spend too much extra time teaching.

Next, we are going to give you some examples of how we can adjust our presses to either full or half court. Diagram 59 illustrates moving our 2-1-2 press to a full-court matchup.

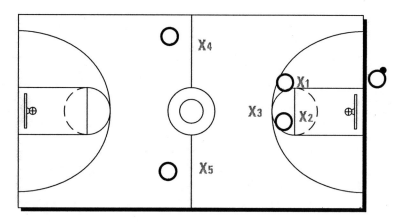

Diagram 59

This is one of the primary ways we will run our full-court press.

X1 AND X2

- Set up on the line and up the line to deny the entry pass.

- They can completely face-guard their offensive matchup and not worry about the pass over their heads.

- If the two guards stack and split, X1 and X2 simply take the one who comes out to their side of the court.

- They switch any crosses by the offensive guards.

- If the ball is entered, they continue to follow the force to the sideline and push the dribbler into a trap at half court.

X3

- Plays behind the front line of offensive players and takes away any lob over the top of the defensive guards.

- This should force the offensive players to have to beat X1 and X2 to get open toward the baseline.

- If the ball is successfully inbounded, X3 drops to the middle and matches up.

X4 and X5

- They start on the line and up the line and deny any flash cuts toward the ball by the two offensive players downcourt.

- Once the ball is entered, they prepare to trap at half court as the guards are forcing to the sideline.

This type of defensive adjustment is particularly effective after a breakaway basket or as a surprise. It often makes different offensive players handle the ball. Many times the ball will immediately be given back to the inbounder after he steps in bounds, since he is not guarded in the initial matchup. With this press, we can easily determine which of the guards we let receive the ball and which one we do not want to have it.

FULL-COURT PRESSURE—TRAP THE FIRST PASS

This trap is very similar to a diamond press. Diagram 60 shows the alignment and trap that occurs on the first pass inbounds. We use this press for the element of surprise and to make someone other than the point guard handle the ball.

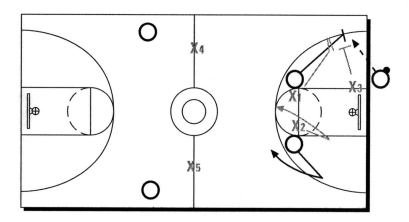

Diagram 60

X1 and X2
- Take a stance that influences their man as far into the corner to catch the ball as possible.

- The closer to the baseline, the better.

- If their matchup receives the inbound pass, they have the outside responsibility on the trap with X3.

- If X1 is involved in the trap, X2 drops to the middle to deny the ball to anyone cutting to that area.

X3
- Covers the inbounder and follows his entry pass to trap with either guard.

- Once there, he is responsible for taking away the split and the dribble to the middle.

- After the first trap, he relocates to the middle of the 2-1-2 press.

X4 and X5
- Start on the line and up the line to deny any direct pass or flash.

HALF-COURT ROTATIONS VS. A 2-1-2 OFFENSIVE SET

Diagram 61 illustrates the matchup press used at half court against a 2-1-2 alignment.

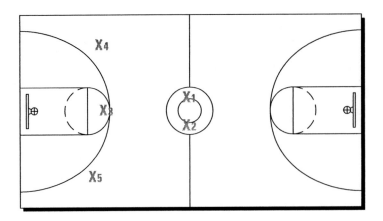

Diagram 61

The only differences are the pickup point by the guards and how they initiate the pressure. The guards run what we call a "wedge." This is where they stand in the half-court circle, with their backs almost facing each other, wedging the offensive attack toward the sideline. These stances by the guards "fan" the ball to the side, where all of our rules for the full-court press remain intact.

This is amore conservative type of pressure because the area being defended is much smaller, and the drops are correspondingly much shorter. Wedging the guards at half court will also prevent the offense from reversing the ball back and forth and running your big people from side to side with each reversal.

CHAPTER 10

Keys to Having a Great Matchup Press

1. Scout your opposition and prepare a plan to take away their primary plan of attack against the press.

2. Understand their personnel and know who you want to handle the ball and who you do not want to have it.

3. Encourage their non-players to make plays—not their players.

4. Put their non–decision makers in situations where they are making the decisions.

5. Match up with their initial alignment and then follow your plan to push the ball toward either the sideline or the middle.

6. Fundamental trapping techniques must be used to make the most of the opportunities we have to trap.

7. Do not let an offensive player split a trap.

8. Do not foul in a trap.

9. As the ball leaves the trap, both defenders must sprint to their next assignment.

10. Every time there is a trap, we should have two people anticipating the pass out of the trap and one protecting the basket.

11. If we do not give up easy baskets, pressing can be effective without causing turnovers by simply fatiguing the other team.

12. Keep constant pressure on the other team.

13. Adjust your press so it is able to either slow the game down or speed it up.

14. Be ready to adjust your press to different levels on the floor so you can see where it may be most effective.

15. Keep pushing the ball farther into the box.

16. Take advantage of energy spurts in the game; when they come, go for the big run.

17. Attempt to deny any kind of ball reversal so you can keep the ball-side defenders and the help-side defenders established.

18. Be the aggressor.

SUMMARY

We have had a great deal of success with the matchup press in recent years. Much of our success is due to the quickness of our athletes, but some of the effectiveness can be credited to the techniques and drills used by our coaching staff to teach the fundamentals of the defense. No defense is as devastating as a press. It controls the game, providing a high level of emotion and energy for your players, and affects the mental attitude of your opponent. There are times that the press gets us off to a quick start, and other times it has allowed us to get back into a game after being way behind. You are never out of a game if you can press.

Theoretically, the press is never over until you decide to call it off. Each time, and with each new location of the ball, you simply regroup and go at them again. This type of defense is effective against all types of teams, but particularly against those teams that want to control the tempo of the game. We have been able to press teams, regardless of what their strengths are, by making small adjustments to counter their strengths.

Hopefully, this book has helped to answer most of your questions about our matchup press. We love the consistency it provides us. Our defensive breakdown drills carry over whether we play matchup or man-to-man. This carryover helps our players to be able to react when they are playing, instead of thinking their way through each movement.

Basketball is a game of neuromuscular integration, which is commonly referred to as "muscle memory." You must continue to work to improve your footwork and pursuit angles and rotations and trapping until they become ingrained in your players' neuromuscular system. Your players can then react instinctively in every situation. Repetition is the name of the game in coaching. Our success as coaches often depends on being able to come up with different and unique drills that do the same basic things every day without the players realizing they are doing the same fundamental over and over.

I would like to take this opportunity to thank all the people who have helped me in the formation of my coaching philosophy, my former and present assistants, as well as my father, who coached me in high school. He taught me much more than the game of basketball, and for that, I will be eternally grateful.

Good luck this season. Keep working and caring about this great game.

Bob Huggins is a proven success as a program-builder, recruiter, game strategist and motivator. He has demonstrated this in a myriad of ways since joining the University of Cincinnati in 1989.

Inheriting a team that was short on numbers, Huggins inspired his initial team to a post season tournament and has done so every year since. Coach Huggins has compiled an impressive 247-82 record in his first 10 years at Cincinnati, making him the winningest coach in U. C. history.

For his efforts, Coach Huggins has been awarded many coaching honors, including the Ray Meyer Award as the Conference USA Coach of the Year in 1997 and 1998. He was also Basketball Times' selection for national coach of the year in 1997–'98, and was Playboy magazine's national coach of the year in 1992-'93.

Huggins began his coaching career as a graduate assistant at his alma mater, The University of West Virginia, in 1997. Subsequent coaching stints have included Ohio State (1978–'80), Walsh College (1980–'83), Central Florida (1983), and the University of Akron (1984–'89).

Born in Morgantown, W. Va., Huggins grew up in Gnadenhutten, Ohio where he played high school basketball for his father, Charles Huggins, at Gnadenhutten Indian Valley South. Bob and his wife, June, have two daughters, Jenna and Jacqueline.